BEC Preliminary
Testbuilder

Jake Allsop and Tricia Aspinall

MACMILLAN

Macmillan Education
Between Towns Road, Oxford OX4 3PP
A division of Macmillan Publishers Limited
Companies and representatives throughout the world

ISBN 1 405 01831 3

First published 2004

Original design by Xen Media Ltd
Page layout by eMC Design, www.emcdesign.org.uk
Illustrated by Peter Cornwell and Val Saunders
Cover design by Xen Media Ltd

The authors would like to thank Tanya Whatling and Sarah Curtis
for their help.

The publishers would like to thank Russell Whitehead for his
comments.

Printed and bound in the UK by
Scotprint

2008 2007 2006 2005 2004
10 9 8 7 6 5 4 3 2 1

CONTENTS

Introduction   4

INTRODUCTION

The BEC Preliminary Testbuilder provides students with the information and practice they need to pass BEC Preliminary. It offers teachers and students an encouraging and accessible way to prepare for the exam and may be used as part of a business English course or as a self-access programme for students preparing for the exam on their own. There are four complete practice tests that reflect the content and level of the actual examination. All the tests are of a similar standard and include the themes, topics and vocabulary specified in the BEC Preliminary Syllabus. They are accompanied by an expanded answer key and further practice and guidance sections.

Expanded Key

The main purpose of the expanded keys is to promote confidence and understanding of the demands of the exam. They give students and teachers information about why a particular answer is correct and, when appropriate, there are explanations as to why other options or possible answers are incorrect.

Further Practice and Guidance

Each part of the test is accompanied by one or more further practice and guidance sections. The aim of these sections is to give students more information about how to tackle the particular item types in that part of the test. There are also graduated exercises to enable them to improve their test technique as well as their language skills.

The BEC examination covers the four language skills of reading, writing, listening and speaking. At Preliminary level the reading and writing skills are combined in one question paper.

Reading and Writing (1 hour 30 minutes)

Reading

This test is in seven parts. There is one mark for each question.

Part One

This consists of five short texts, for example, advertisements, business cards, notices. Each text is followed by a multiple-choice question. This part tests your ability to identify or interpret meaning from the context. See page 8 for further practice and guidance.

Part Two

This consists of a short text followed by five questions. The text may be the contents of a directory or book, the plan of an office or a department store, items in a catalogue, etc. The task is to match each question to an appropriate part of the text. This part tests vocabulary and meaning. See page 42 for further practice and guidance.

Part Three

This consists of eight graphs, charts or tables followed by five statements. Each of the statements refers to one of the eight items. The task is to match the statement to the correct item. This part tests your ability to interpret information presented graphically, and to understand trends and changes. See page 45 for further practice and guidance.

Part Four

This consists of a text of 150–200 words followed by seven multiple-choice questions. Each question is a statement, and the task is to decide between three options for each statement: **A** 'Right', **B** 'Wrong' or **C** 'Doesn't say' (when there is not enough information in the text to say). This part tests the ability to identify incorrect information. See page 14 for further practice and guidance.

Part Five

This consists of a text of 300–400 words, taken from a magazine, newspaper, book, etc. The text is followed by six multiple-choice questions. This part tests the ability to extract relevant information, to read for gist and detail, to scan for specific information and to understand the writer's purpose. See page 80 for further practice and guidance.

Part Six

This consists of a text of 125–150 words taken from a magazine article, a leaflet, etc., with fifteen gaps. For each gap there is a multiple choice from which the correct word is to be selected. This part tests your knowledge of grammar and your ability to analyse structural patterns. See page 82 for further practice and guidance.

Part Seven

This consists of two short texts, for example, a memo and an advertisement, and a form to be completed using the information in the texts. The form has five gaps which should be filled with a word, number or short phrase. This part tests your ability to extract relevant information and to complete a form accurately. See page 112 for further practice and guidance.

Writing

The writing test is in two parts:

Part One

The task is to produce an internal company communication in the form of a memo, a note, a message or an email of 30–40 words, based on two or three pieces of information. The information usually says who the writer is, who the recipient is, and then gives the purpose of the written communication. This part tests your ability to communicate briefly and accurately in writing. See pages 23–24 and 114 for further practice and guidance.

Part Two

The task is to produce a piece of business correspondence in the form of a letter, a fax or an email of about 60–80 words, based on a short text. The text usually consists of an advertisement, a leaflet or a letter, often with the writer's notes showing where more information or explanation is required by the writer. This part tests your ability to process information, and then to structure a piece of writing in a way that is accurate in both content and language. See pages 56 and 86 for further practice and guidance.

Listening (40 minutes)

The listening test for BEC Preliminary consists of a series of recorded extracts and a written question paper. All the instructions are on the recording and on the question paper. The test is in four parts and lasts about 30 minutes altogether. Each section is played twice. In the exam itself there is an extra ten minutes to transfer the answers on to a special computer-marked answer sheet. There is one mark for each question.

Part One

This consists of eight short conversations or monologues (when one person is speaking). Each recording is played twice. There are eight multiple-choice questions with three choices or 'options'. These options may be pictures, graphs, charts or short sentences or phrases. This part tests your ability to understand facts such as a name, a time or a place. See pages 28–29 and 119 for further practice and guidance.

Part Two

This consists of a short conversation between two people or a monologue. The recording will last about one and a half minutes. On the question paper there is a form, a table, a chart or a set of notes with seven gaps. The task is to fill in the missing information which may be a date, a price, a percentage or figures. This part tests your ability to listen out for factual information. See page 61 for further practice and guidance.

Part Three

This consists of a recording of one person speaking. Usually they are giving a speech or a talk about something. On the question paper there is a set of notes with seven gaps. The task is to fill in the missing information with one or two words. This part tests your ability to listen out for specific details. See page 63 for further practice and guidance.

Part Four

This consists of a longer listening text which may be an interview or discussion between two or more speakers. The recording lasts for about three minutes and it is played twice. On the question paper there are eight multiple-choice questions. This tests your ability to pick out specific details and to show a general understanding (or the *gist*) of the interview or discussion, including any opinions the speakers may express. See page 93 for further practice and guidance.

Speaking (12 minutes)

The speaking test is taken in pairs and, occasionally, with three candidates. There are two examiners. One of them (the interlocutor) will speak to you and lead you through the tasks. The other examiner just listens.

The test is in three parts:

Part One

In this part the interlocutor talks to each of you in turn and asks general questions about where you live and work or what you are studying or what you do in your spare time. The questions will be slightly different for each of you and you will not always be asked them in the same order. This part of the test lasts about two minutes.

This part tests how well you can talk about yourself and whether you can give information about your home, your job and your studies. The examiners will also expect you to know how to agree and disagree about things and to say what things you prefer. See page 35 for further practice and guidance.

Part Two

In this part you will be asked to speak for about one minute on a business topic. This is called a 'mini-presentation'. You will be able to choose from two topics. Each topic is written on a card with three points about it. You can talk about some or all of these points. Once you have chosen your topic, you have one minute to prepare. You need to speak for at least 45 seconds.

After each of you has finished speaking, the interlocutor will ask the other candidate(s) a question about what you have been talking about. This part of the test lasts for about five minutes. This tests how well you present some basic ideas and how you structure what you are going to say. See page 67 for further practice and guidance.

Part Three

In this part the interlocutor introduces a situation for you to discuss. There are pictures or short notes to help you. You are asked to discuss the situation together. You have about two minutes to do this and then the interlocutor will ask you more questions about it. This tests how well you talk together, in particular, how you express opinions and agree and disagree with each other. See pages 97 and 126 for further practice and guidance.

TEST ONE

READING AND WRITING 1 hour 30 minutes

PART ONE

Questions 1–5

- *Look at questions 1–5.*

- *In each question, which sentence is correct?*

- *For each question, mark one letter (A, B or C).*

Example:

0 | Susan's arriving at 8.45pm tomorrow. Can you collect her from the station? |

Susan arrives at

A quarter to eight tomorrow morning.

B quarter to nine tomorrow evening.

C quarter to nine tomorrow morning.

The correct answer is **B**, so mark your answer sheet like this:

---

1 | **For all personal calls except emergencies, please use payphone in Reception.** |

A Staff may use office phones in case of emergency.

B Emergency calls must be made on the payphone.

C Reception deals with emergency calls.

2

Photocopiers	Pages per minute	Input tray	Copy time (first copy)
AL-1045	12	250 sheets	9.6 seconds
D135	14	150 sheets	10.5 seconds
D155X	19	400 sheets	8.4 seconds

Which is the fastest photocopier?

A AL-1045

B D135

C D155X

3

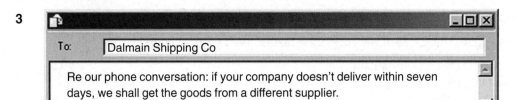

To: Dalmain Shipping Co

Re our phone conversation: if your company doesn't deliver within seven days, we shall get the goods from a different supplier.

This means that Dalmain Shipping Co must

A   get the goods from another company.

B   phone to confirm when the goods will be delivered.

C   deliver the goods on time or lose the order.

4   Diary for Ms Caroline Carter

Mon	10	*Flight Lisboa-Rio, transfer to hotel*	Mon	17	*Visit to port facilities*
Tues	11	*Meeting with Sr Ribeiro*	Tues	18	*Meeting with Sr Ribeiro*
Wed	12	*Factory visits*	Wed	19	*Flight Rio-Lisboa*
Thurs	13	*Transfer by car to Amanha*			
Fri	14	*Board meeting*			
Sat	15	*Free day*			
Sun	16	*Free day*			

Excluding travel, on how many days is Caroline working?

A   5

B   6

C   8

5

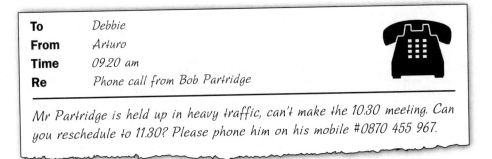

To	*Debbie*
From	*Arturo*
Time	*09.20 am*
Re	*Phone call from Bob Partridge*

Mr Partridge is held up in heavy traffic, can't make the 10.30 meeting. Can you reschedule to 11.30? Please phone him on his mobile #0870 455 967.

Bob Partridge wants to

A   phone Debbie on his mobile.

B   change the time of the meeting.

C   speak to Arturo.

Before you check your answers, go to page 8.

EXAM INFORMATION

In Part One of the reading test there are always five short texts to read. The text may be:

- a notice, label or short text giving information
- an instruction, a warning, etc
- all or part of a diagram or table
- an advertisement
- a business card
- a timetable
- pages of a diary
- part or all of a fax, email, phone message.

For each text, there is a question with three choices or 'options'. Only one of the options is correct. This part of the test is designed to see how carefully you read so that you can match the facts in the text to one of the three options.

A DETAILED STUDY

1   Read questions **1–5** on pages 6–7and decide which of the categories above each text belongs to.

1   _____

2   _____

3   _____

4   _____

5   _____

2   Read the texts again and answer these questions by writing **T** (for true) or **F** (for false) in the table.

		True	False
Question 1			
1	An emergency may be something personal.		
2	There is a payphone in Reception.		
Question 2			
3	D135 is the fastest machine.		
4	These machines can copy between 12 and 19 pages a minute.		
Question 3			
5	This email is about sending goods to Dalmain in good time.		
6	The writer has decided to get the goods from another supplier.		
Question 4			
7	Caroline is going to Rio on business.		
8	Caroline will travel from Amanha back to Rio by car.		
Question 5			
9	Arturo needs to speak to Debbie.		
10	Mr Partridge phoned from his car.		

Now check your answers to these questions and then look back at your answers to Part One of the reading test.

PART TWO

Questions 6–10

- *Look at the items below. This is a page from a catalogue of office supplies.*

- *For questions 6–10 on the next page, decide which item (A–H) would suit each member of staff.*

- *For each question, mark the correct letter (A–H).*

- *Do not use any letter more than once.*

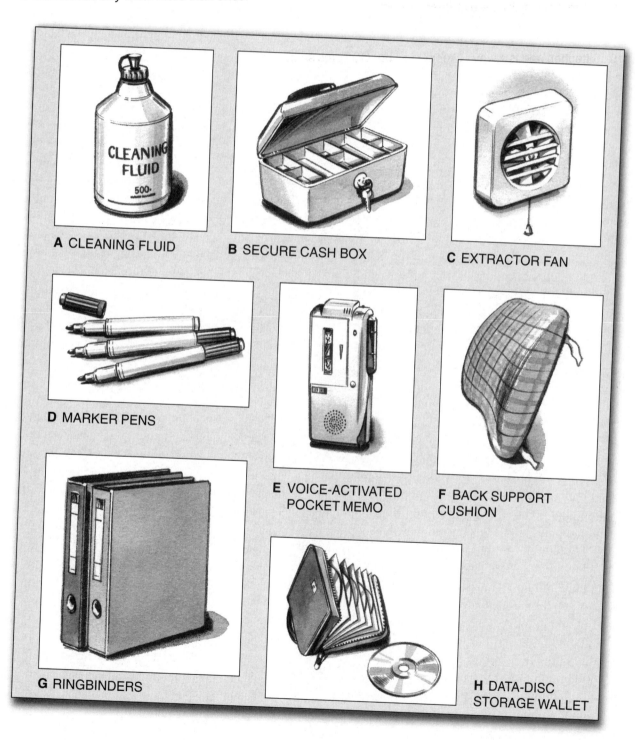

A CLEANING FLUID

B SECURE CASH BOX

C EXTRACTOR FAN

D MARKER PENS

E VOICE-ACTIVATED POCKET MEMO

F BACK SUPPORT CUSHION

G RINGBINDERS

H DATA-DISC STORAGE WALLET

6   Yunhua is collecting money and needs somewhere safe to put it.

7   Lee gets a lot of pain through sitting too long at his computer.

8   Pauline and Mary are complaining that they can't breathe because of the dust in the office.

9   Michel has spilt coffee all over his desk.

10   Stephen needs a way of keeping all our CDRoms safe.

PART THREE
Questions 11–15

- *Look at the chart below. It shows the quarterly turnover figures for eight wholesalers, lettered **A–H**.*

- *Which year in the chart does each sentence (**11–15**) below describe?*

- *For each sentence, mark one letter (**A–H**).*

- *Do not use any letter more than once.*

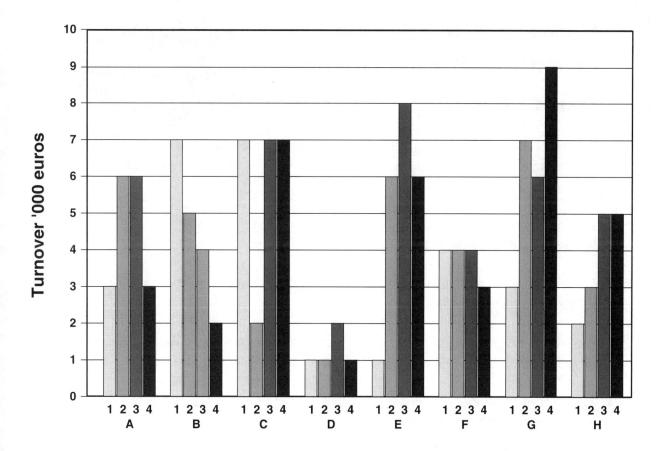

11   One of the poorest years on record, with sales picking up briefly in the third quarter.

12   A very uneven year, which was saved by good results in the middle two quarters.

13   After a poor start, sales were at record levels with the fourth quarter beating all records.

14   A very good year except for a disastrous fall in business between April and June.

15   After the worst start to the year in living memory, sales reached an amazing peak in the third quarter before falling back a little.

PART FOUR
Questions 16–22

- *Read the advertisement below for an online vehicle spares service.*

- *Are the sentences **16–22** on the opposite page right or wrong? If there is not enough information to answer 'Right' or 'Wrong', choose 'Doesn't say'.*

- *For each sentence **16–22**, mark one letter (**A, B** or **C**).*

Kelly Auto Spares
Order Vehicle Spare
Parts online!

It's as easy as that!

Download our easy-to-use program* from **www.kellyautospares.co.uk**. The software
is free: there's just a one-off registration fee of €25, which we will refund with your first
order.

We stock spares for all leading domestic and foreign makes, including: Ford, GM,
Volkswagen, Fiat, Peugeot, Toyota, etc.

Online orders are confirmed by email, with expected delivery time. Delivery is usually
within 48 hours of receipt of order.

You will be lucky to find a cheaper supplier than *KellyAutoSpares*. We offer discounts
on spares for all leading domestic makes, and for many foreign makes too.

There's no minimum size of order. We will deliver, at standard parcel-post rates, orders
of any value, from €10 to €1,000,000!

You can pay online by credit card using our SECURE payment system. We make a 5%
handling charge for payment by cheque.

If you have problems, visit our website and click on 'Online Support'. You can also
phone our helpline on 01678 505050, weekdays
between 8am and 6pm.

*System requirements: IBM-compatible PC,
Windows 98 or later, 5Mb hard disk space.
Mac users, email
KellyAutoSpares@KAS.co.uk for
instructions.*

16   *KellyAutoSpares* will accept very small orders.

    A   Right   **B**   Wrong   **C**   Doesn't say

17   The program costs €25.

    A   Right   **B**   Wrong   **C**   Doesn't say

18   It will cost you more if you pay by cheque.

    A   Right   **B**   Wrong   **C**   Doesn't say

19   Goods ordered online (i.e. on the website) can be paid for COD.

    A   Right   **B**   Wrong   **C**   Doesn't say

20   The software needs to be modified for use with Mac computers.

    A   Right   **B**   Wrong   **C**   Doesn't say

21   *KellyAutoSpares* carries spares for all popular vehicles.

    A   Right   **B**   Wrong   **C**   Doesn't say

22   You can get help by visiting *KellyAutoSpares*' website.

    A   Right   **B**   Wrong   **C**   Doesn't say

Before you check your answers, go to pages 14–15.

EXAM INFORMATION

Part Four of the reading test has a text which gives information in various forms such as:

- an advertisement: offering a product or a service
- a letter: applying for a job, asking about a course, etc
- a magazine/newspaper article: describing a product, service, event, person, etc
- promotional literature: describing a new product, etc
- a report: reporting an event, a conference, etc
- minutes: recording what happened at a meeting.

After the text there are seven statements followed by three options: *Right*, *Wrong* and *Doesn't say*. *Doesn't say* means that you cannot say if the statement is true or false, because the text doesn't contain any information about that statement.

This part of the test is to see how carefully you read the text, and how well you are able to match each statement to information in the text.

A DETAILED STUDY

1   The questions below will help you understand the text better and make sure you answer the correct options for questions **16–22**.

　　1   What is the company's business?

　　　　They supply _____.

　　2   How can you get the software?

　　　　You can _____.

　　3   Which makes are covered by their service?

　　　　They cover _____.

　　4   What is delivery time?

　　　　They will usually deliver _____.

　　5   Will you have to pay the full list price for items?

　　　　They offer _____.

　　6   What is the smallest size of order they will accept?

　　　　They will accept _____.

　　7   Where can you get advice if you need it?

　　　　The company has _____.

　　8   Will the software work on any PC computer?

　　　　Yes, but you must have _____.

2   The difference between a *Wrong* statement and a *Doesn't say* statement is often quite difficult to decide. Look at these statements and decide whether they are *Wrong* or *Doesn't say*.

    1   Kelly Autospares is an American company.

    2   They are cheaper than other supplies of autospares.

    3   The method of payment method is cash or cheque.

    4   Mac users cannot use the computer system.

    5   The company deals only with domestic customers.

    6   You must register the software with your first order.

    7   The software works better in Windows 2000 or later.

Now check your answers and then look back at your answers to Part Four of the reading test.

PART FIVE

Questions 23–28

- *Read the text below about an agency that promotes business cooperation in the EU.*

- *For each question 23–28 on the opposite page, choose the correct answer.*

- *Mark one letter (A, B or C).*

Interprise

No, it isn't the word 'enterprise' spelled wrongly! *Interprise* is an EU agency that encourages cross-border business cooperation. It is a like a 'dating agency' that tries to match people who are looking for love. *Interprise* helps businesses to find partners in other countries to join in trading or distribution arrangements.

The agency's task is to set up face-to-face meetings with business counterparts from other countries. This is how it works. The agency gets a request from a company, known as the 'host company' (like a person who hosts a party), to help it find overseas companies. The host company creates a theme, that is, to say exactly what it wants. The Agency then helps it to team up with more host companies from at least two other EU regions who are looking for similar partners.

The Agency then publicizes the coming event to attract as many 'guests' (visitors) as possible, that is, companies who might be interested in partnerships with the host companies. To do this, *Interprise* produces an '*Interprise* Catalogue' in which the host companies describe themselves and say what kind of partner they are looking for, for example, 'a partner in Germany to distribute our products'. The EU covers part of the running costs of the event, up to 70,000 euros. In order to reach as many people as possible, the agency works through local Chambers of Commerce, who in turn publicize the event to their own members. Each Chamber of Commerce is expected to bring at least fifteen companies. A recent *Interprise* event had 150 host companies and over 200 registered visitors.

But *Interprise* is not an easy idea to 'sell'. It is not a trade fair in the usual sense. The average trade fair is like window-shopping: firms set out their goods, and visitors look round to see if there's anything they want. With *Interprise*, everything is carefully arranged in advance. Foreign companies want a full programme of meetings – and with the right people. It is too early to say if *Interprise* is a success, but comments from both host companies and visitors have been very positive. 'I've a pocketful of business cards and have made several useful contacts.' 'Great! We have met some firms that are really interested in becoming distributors.' Of course, they might have made useful contacts at an ordinary trade fair, except that it would have been only by chance.

23   What is *Interprise*?

    A   another word for 'enterprise'

    B   a dating agency

    C   a way of matching companies

24   The purpose of an *Interprise* event is to

    A   buy and sell products.

    B   meet others with similar interests.

    C   travel to other countries.

25   *Interprise* catalogues are distributed

    A   during an *Interprise* event.

    B   after an *Interprise* event.

    C   before an *Interprise* event.

26   The role of Chambers of Commerce is to

    A   welcome visitors to the event.

    B   find the host companies.

    C   organize the *Interprise* event.

27   An *Interprise* event is different from a trade fair because

    A   people meet face to face.

    B   meetings are planned before the event.

    C   the EU pays for part of the running costs.

28   Host companies are happy with an *Interprise* event if they have

    A   made useful contacts.

    B   promoted their business.

    C   distributed their product.

PART SIX
Questions 29–40

- *Read the article below about working as a secretary in Hong Kong.*

- *Choose the correct word to fill each gap, from **A, B** or **C** on the opposite page.*

- *For each question **29–40**, mark one letter (**A, B** or **C**).*

Secretaries in Hong Kong

Secretaries in Hong Kong work hard. They work a 12-hour day, and are
expected to work five and a half days **(29)** .... week. They need good
qualifications, and **(30)** .... be able to speak and read English **(31)** .... well as
Cantonese or Mandarin. Most of **(32)** .... are university graduates, so working
as a secretary is **(33)** .... as a 'fill in' job **(34)** .... they can find something better.

Most **(35)** .... between £17,000 and £22,000 pa, and get **(36)** .... more than
eleven days' annual holiday. You really have to work hard **(37)** .... your money
in Hong Kong! And it is very expensive to live there. Employers provide
medical insurance, but it only covers **(38)** .... to 50% of the costs. A very small
apartment can **(39)** .... £2,000 per month rent. Cars are expensive, and petrol is
so dear that **(40)** .... very well-paid people use public transport.

29	**A** the	**B** a	**C** by
30	**A** need	**B** must	**C** can
31	**A** so	**B** and	**C** as
32	**A** them	**B** him	**C** her
33	**A** seeing	**B** see	**C** seen
34	**A** until	**B** when	**C** while
35	**A** win	**B** gain	**C** earn
36	**A** any	**B** some	**C** no
37	**A** for	**B** with	**C** to
38	**A** in	**B** up	**C** next
39	**A** cost	**B** costs	**C** costing
40	**A** even	**B** also	**C** just

PART SEVEN

Questions 41–45

- *Read the memo and email below.*

- *Complete the form on the opposite page.*

- *Write a word or phrase (in CAPITAL LETTERS) or a number on lines 41–45.*

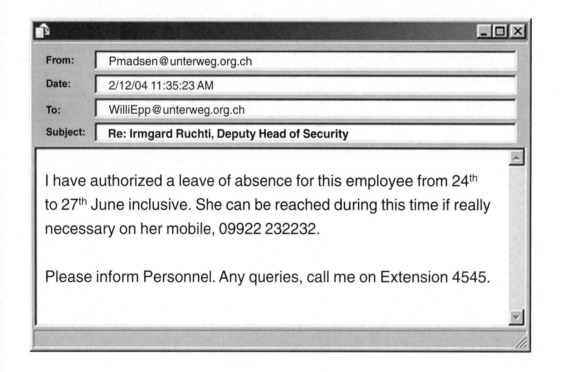

Memo

To: Rolf

From: Willi

Date: 02/12/04

I just received this email from Peter Madsen, Head of Security, authorizing a leave of absence for the Deputy Head of Security. It seems she has to go for an interview – a senior post with SafeHands Security! Lucky woman! Could you send a file note to Personnel?

From:	Pmadsen@unterweg.org.ch
Date:	2/12/04 11:35:23 AM
To:	WilliEpp@unterweg.org.ch
Subject:	**Re: Irmgard Ruchti, Deputy Head of Security**

I have authorized a leave of absence for this employee from 24th to 27th June inclusive. She can be reached during this time if really necessary on her mobile, 09922 232232.

Please inform Personnel. Any queries, call me on Extension 4545.

File Note

From: RS

To: Personnel

Re: <u>Leave of Absence</u>

Employee's name   **(41)** ....

Department   **(42)** ....

Dates requested   **(43)** ....

Reason for absence   **(44)** ....

Emergency contact no.   **(45)** ....

Authorized by   *J Madsen,* *Head of Security*

WRITING

PART ONE

Question 46

- *You are the office manager of a large company, and you want to attend an exhibition of the latest office equipment. You need permission from your boss to attend.*

- *Write your boss a **memo**:*

  - *explaining why you think the exhibition is important*

  - *requesting permission to attend*

  - *saying where and when the exhibition takes place.*

- *Write **30–40** words.*

MEMO

To: Tansu Ordek

From:

Date:

Re: **Office Equipment Exhibition**

....

....

....

....

....

....

....

....

....

Before you write your memo, go to pages 23–24.

EXAM INFORMATION

In Part One of the writing test you have to write a short piece of about 30–40 words, in the form of:

- a memo
- an email
- a fax message
- a short note.

The topics include events, such as:

- a meeting
- a conference
- an exhibition
- travel
- a training course.

You are usually asked to do three or four things, such as:

A   giving or confirming information

B   asking for permission

C   explaining what has happened or will happen

D   saying why something has or has not been done

E   apologizing

F   making a suggestion

G   inviting someone

H   thanking someone

I   making a complaint

J   offering or accepting services

Look at these phrases and say which of the categories (**A–J**) each one belongs to.

1   ... we would like you to attend our annual company dinner ...

2   ... the goods were not delivered because the delivery van broke down ...

3   ... I will be away from my desk until 27 September ...

4   ... we are very sorry for any inconvenience caused by the delay ...

5   ... would it be all right if I worked from home for the next two weeks?

6   ... we are very grateful for your help in this matter ...

7   ... your receptionist was very rude and even put the phone down on me ...

8   ... the warehouse has burned down ...

9   ... it might be a good idea to get Carla in Accounts to check your figures ...

10   ... so I believe our organization has the expertise to help you.

A DETAILED STUDY

Read this model memo and answer the questions.

MEMO

To: Nuria Gomez
From: Pau Pujols
Date: 12 April
Re: **Kitchen Equipment Annual Trade Fair**

This year the fair is in Geneva, from 10–14 May inclusive. As we are to equip several new restaurants, I should attend to learn about the latest products. Registration is SF150. I don't need accommodation as I have family there.

(39 words)

1   How often does the fair take place?

2   Is it always held in the same place?

3   How many days does it last?

4   Why is his attendance at the exhibition important?

5   Where in the memo does he ask permission?

6   How can he save on costs?

Now write your own answer to question 46 in Part One of the writing test. Remember to check for grammar and spelling mistakes.

PART TWO

Question 47

- *Read this fax inquiring about your company's services.*

ACD Financial Services
Fax

To:
From: Ali Bardak
Re: Your advertisement in Training Quarterly
Date:
Pages: 1

Further to your advertisement in the current issue of Training Quarterly, we are interested in your in-house training services.

We are an expanding company and have recently taken on several new office staff who will need training in clerical skills.

If you think you can help us, please get in touch with me.

Tel: (direct) 216 343 7600
Fax: 216 343 7610

- *Write a **fax** to Ali Bardak:*

  - *acknowledging his fax and expressing interest*

  - *asking which clerical skills he is referring to*

  - *asking for more information about numbers of staff*

  - *suggesting a meeting.*

- *Write **60–80** words.*

- *Do not include postal addresses.*

LISTENING 40 minutes

PART ONE

Questions 1–8

Before you answer questions 1–8, go to pages 28–29.

- *For questions **1–8** you will hear eight short recordings.*

- *For each question, mark one letter (**A**, **B** or **C**) for the most suitable picture or phrase.*

Example:

What did the sign say?

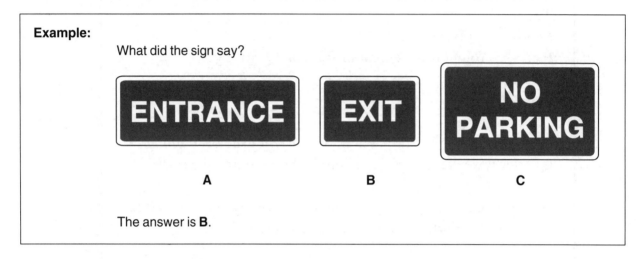

A   B   C

The answer is **B**.

---

1   What time is the woman's appointment?

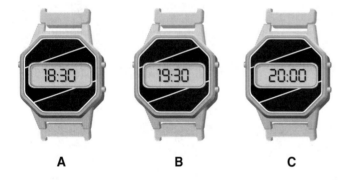

A   B   C

2   Where will the company's headquarters be?

- **A**   Dublin
- **B**   Belfast
- **C**   Cork

3   What must the passenger for the flight to Munich do next?

   A   Go to the information desk.

   B   Go to the check-in desk.

   C   Go to the gate to board the plane.

4   Where is Mr Fleming?

A   B   C

5   Which is the correct chart?

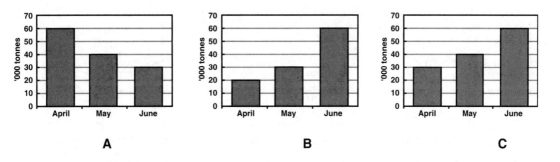

A   B   C

6   What is the exchange rate today?

   A   €1 = $1.00

   B   €1 = $0.97

   C   €1 = $0.93

7   What is the woman going to collect?

   A   a computer

   B   a monitor

   C   a printer

8   Who does the woman need to speak to?

   A   the manager

   B   the operator

   C   Customer Services

PART ONE: QUESTIONS USING GRAPHS AND CHARTS

Remember

- Before you listen to the recording, study each of the three graphs or charts.
- Decide what each graph or chart is showing.
- Take note of what is written on the horizontal and vertical axes.

Look at each graph (taken from tests 1–4) and match the statements **i–iii** to the correct graph, **A**, **B** or **C**.

1

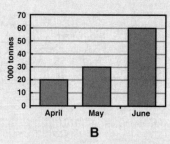
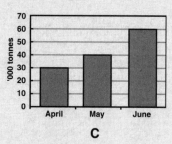

| A | B | C |

i   In the last three months we have seen output increase from 20 to 60 thousand tonnes.

ii   In the last three months we have seen output increase from 30 to 60 tonnes.

iii In the last three months we have seen output decrease from 60 to 30 tonnes.

2

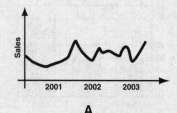
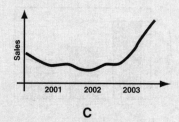

| A | B | C |

i   Since 2001, when sales were really poor, there has been a steady, if slow, improvement.

ii   Sales were steady for two years but since 2002 there has been a significant improvement.

iii Since 2001 sales have been up and down.

3

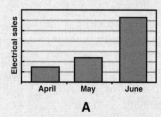
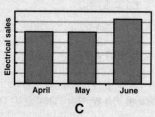

| A | B | C |

i   Electrical goods didn't sell well in May but April and June were good months.

ii   April and May were good months for electrical goods and June has been outstanding.

iii Electrical goods have sold well in June but May wasn't great and April was even worse.

4

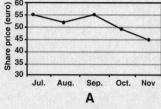
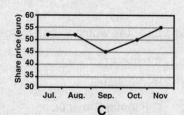

| A | B | C |

i   Share prices have risen by ten euros since September.

ii   Share prices have fallen by ten euros since September.

iii Share prices continued to fall reaching a low of 40 euros in September.

EXAM INFORMATION

In Part One of the listening test there are always eight short conversations or monologues (when only one person is speaking) to listen to. There is a question for each one with three choices or 'options'. These options may be pictures, graphs, charts or short sentences or phrases.

This part of the listening test is testing your ability to understand facts such as a name, a time or a place. You will need to listen very carefully to each conversation or monologue. You will hear each piece twice.

A DETAILED STUDY

1   Before you listen to Part One, read through the questions **1–8** and look carefully at the options.

2   For each question, decide if you are going to be listening for:
   - a time
   - a date   1 _____   5 _____
   - a place
   - a trend (in a graph or chart)   2 _____   6 _____
   - an object
   - a number   3 _____   7 _____
   - an action
   - a person.   4 _____   8 _____

3   Listen to the conversations or monologues and answer these questions by writing **T** (for true) or **F** (for false) in the table.

Question 1		True	False
1	The woman can't go to the cinema tonight.		
2	The film starts at half-past seven.		
Question 2			
3	The woman is moving to Belfast.		
4	A new store is opening in Cork.		
Question 3			
5	Herr Frank is going to Munich.		
6	He is in a hurry to catch his flight.		
Question 4			
7	The woman knows where Mr Fleming is.		
Question 5			
8	Steel production was very good last year.		
9	Thirty thousand tonnes of steel was produced by the end of December.		
Question 6			
10	At the moment the euro is worth one dollar.		
Question 7			
11	The repair company has fixed the woman's lap-top.		
12	The company will deliver this afternoon.		
Question 8			
13	The woman has lost a parcel.		
14	The operator is trying to help the woman.		

Now you are ready to listen again to Part One of the listening test and answer questions 1–8.

PART TWO

Questions 9–15

- *Look at the notes below.*

- *Some information is missing.*

- *You will hear a woman discussing a programme for some interviews.*

- *For each question 9–15, fill in the missing information in the numbered space using a **time**, **numbers** or **letters**.*

Interview Programme
24 May 2004

• •

Number of interviewees: (9) ....

Time of arrival: (10) ....

Interviews begin at: (11) ....

Interviews last for approx: (12) .... minutes

Tests in the board room with: (13) Nina ....

Lunch between: (14) .... and

                                 ....

Amount of petty cash for expenses: (15) ....

PART THREE
Questions 16–22

- *Look at the notes about an agricultural company.*

- *Some information is missing.*

- *You will hear part of a presentation by the managing director of Agriproducts.*

- *For each question **16–22**, fill in the missing information in the numbered space using **one** or **two** words.*

AGRIPRODUCTS PLC

Agriproducts began in: (16) ....

Managing director previously worked as: (17) ....

First products to be marketed were: (18) .... and food products for animals

First business premises in small town in England.

Advantages: lots of space and land (19) ....

Disadvantages: not close to (20) .... or ....

First export market: (21) ....

Next project is to test the market for organic produce in:
(22) ....

PART FOUR
Questions 23–30

- *Listen to this interview with the manager of a beauty salon.*

- *For each question **23–30**, mark one letter (**A**, **B** or **C**) for the correct answer.*

23 Why does the interviewer think Sharon is a good manager?

    A She seems a very happy person.

    B She is an excellent beautician.

    C She can do several things at once.

24 Why does Sharon think she is a good manager?

    A She gets on well with her staff.

    B She watches her staff carefully.

    C She tells her staff what to do.

25 How did she become a manager?

    A She did a management course.

    B Her boss recommended her for the job.

    C The directors asked her to manage the salon.

26 Who owns the salon she manages?

    A Sharon

    B her husband

    C her father

27   When did the salon open?

   A   January

   B   February

   C   April

28   How many people work in the salon?

   A   two

   B   three

   C   five

29   Why is it important for Sharon to know her customers well?

   A   Because they need to trust her.

   B   Because her products are expensive.

   C   Because she spends a lot of time with them.

30   Why does Sharon think her job is a bit like being a doctor?

   A   She makes people feel better about themselves.

   B   She tries to help people with their problems.

   C   She spends a lot of time listening to her customers.

SPEAKING 12 minutes

PART ONE   (ABOUT 2 MINUTES)

In this part of the test the examiner (interlocutor) will ask each of you some questions about where you work or study, where you live or what you do in your free time. Here are some sample questions:

- Where do you live?/Where do you come from?
- What do you like about living there?
- Where would you prefer to live?
- Why is that?
- Do you have any hobbies?
- Could you tell me about …?
- Which hobby would you like to spend more time on?

Now go to pages 35–36.

PART TWO   (ABOUT 5 MINUTES)

In this part of the test you are asked to give a 'mini presentation'. You have a choice of topic such as those below and you have one minute to prepare what you are going to say. After you have spoken, the examiner will ask your partner to say something about what you have said. After you have listened to your partner's presentation, the examiner will ask you to say something about what your partner has said.

Prompt Card (a)   *(Given to Candidate A, and a copy to Candidate B)*

> **A: WHAT IS IMPORTANT WHEN ...?**
>
> **Organizing a meeting**
>
> - Location
>
> - Time and date
>
> - Availability

Prompt Card (b)   *(Given to Candidate B, and a copy to Candidate A)*

> **B: WHAT IS IMPORTANT WHEN ...?**
>
> **Choosing an applicant for a job**
>
> - Experience
>
> - Qualifications
>
> - Personality

EXAM INFORMATION

In Part One of the speaking test the interlocutor talks to each of you in turn and asks general questions about where you live and work or what you are studying or what you do in your spare time. The questions will be slightly different for each of you and you will not always be asked them in the same order. This part of the test lasts about two minutes.

The aim of this part of the test is to see how well you can talk about yourself and whether you can give information about your home, your job and your studies. The examiners will also expect you to know how to agree and disagree about things and to say what things you prefer.

You will be asked some very simple questions which you will not find difficult to answer but remember:

- Listen to the question carefully.
- Don't rush.
- Speak clearly.
- Give the answer to the question you have been asked.
- Don't speak for too long but try not to just say *yes* or *no.*
- If possible, don't just give one-word answers.

> **Example:**   Where do you come from?
> *Pavia. It's a small town in the north of Italy.*

A DETAILED STUDY

1   Here are some questions and suggested answers. Which do you think is the best answer, **A** or **B**? Give a reason for your choice.

Example: Where do you come from?
A   Tallinn.
B   Tallinn. It's the capital city of Estonia.

*B is the best because it is a more complete answer. It shows that you understand the question **and** that you can produce more language.*

1   What do you like about living there?

   A   Well, I have plenty of friends there and we have a good time.

   B   I don't know, really, but I like it.

2   Where would you prefer to live?

   A   I would prefer to live in another place. My sister lives in France.

   B   I think I would like to live in a city like Rome. It sounds like an exciting place.

3   Do you have any hobbies?

   A   Yes. I have many, many hobbies. I like basketball.

   B   Yes, I do. My favourite hobby is watching birds. I think this is quite unusual in Italy.

4   Which hobby would you like to spend more time on?

   A   I would like to spend more time practising the piano. I only practise at weekends.

   B   I don't have any time. I have to work long hours in my job.

2   Choose a sentence **A–G** to add to each reply to give a fuller answer. Two sentences do not fit any of the replies.

1   Are you a student?

*No.*_____

2   What are you studying?

I'm studying English. _____

3   Do you like playing sport?

Yes, I do. _____

4   What do you dislike about your job?

Mainly the early hours. _____

5   What would you like to change about your job?

The pay. _____

A   I find it very difficult to wake up in the morning.

B   I think my job is quite a hard one so I would like to earn more!

C   I used to be but now I work for a small engineering company in Zurich.

D   My favourite activity is tennis. I like to play tennis with my friends after work.

E   I prefer to listen to music or go to the cinema.

F   Next year I hope to get a more interesting job abroad.

G   I am studying business management so speaking the language is very important for me.

Now look again at the sample questions in Part One of the speaking test.

PART THREE (ABOUT 5 MINUTES)

The examiner will describe a situation to you and give you some pictures or a few sentences to help you. You have 30 seconds to look at the prompt card and two minutes to discuss the situation. The examiner will then ask you some more questions about the situation.

Here is an example of a situation:

You have been asked to look after an important visitor who is visiting your company. Talk together for about two minutes about the different things you will need to arrange before they arrive. Decide which three things are the most important.

Here are some pictures to help you:

TEST TWO

READING AND WRITING 1 hour 30 minutes

PART ONE
Questions 1–5

- *Look at questions **1–5**.*

- *In each question, which sentence is correct?*

- *For each question, mark one letter (**A, B** or **C**).*

Example:

0 | *Susan's arriving at 8.45pm tomorrow. Can you collect her from the station?* |

Susan arrives at

A   quarter to eight tomorrow morning.

B   quarter to nine tomorrow evening.

C   quarter to nine tomorrow morning.

The correct answer is **B**, so mark your answer sheet like this:

1

> # Notice to all Staff
> **Confirm your summer holiday
> dates with your Department
> Supervisor before entering them
> on the Holiday List.**

Holiday dates are confirmed once they have been

A   added to the Holiday List.

B   checked with other staff in the department.

C   agreed by your superior.

2

Findit **Accommodation Agency**

We can provide:

- bedsits, flats, houses
- furnished or unfurnished
- long or short lets
- all areas within the city

Call 0182 58 58 00   Or visit www.findit.com

This agency would be used by someone who wanted to

A   rent a furnished apartment for a year.

B   buy a house in the city.

C   find hotel accommodation within the city.

3

Warning: Nibbletreat Biscuits

Packets of this product dated 01-30 June have been withdrawn for health reasons. For a refund, bring your receipt.

You can get a refund if

A   you show your receipt.

B   you return the biscuits to the store.

C   the biscuits made you ill.

4

Joe, best routing for your trip London to Anchorage, with stopover in Ottawa is:

	depart/arrive
London HRW– Ottawa	1500/1745
Ottawa – Toronto	1400/1506
Toronto – Vancouver	1600/1815
Vancouver – Anchorage	2000/2230

Joe will need to spend a night in

A   Vancouver.

B   Toronto.

C   Ottawa.

5

We enclose a stamped addressed envelope for your reply.

This means

A   enclose a stamped addressed envelope with your reply.

B   send your reply in the enclosed envelope.

C   there is no need to enclose a reply.

PART TWO

Questions 6–10

Before you answer questions 6–10, go to page 42.

- *Look at the office plan below. It shows the various sections of a small consultancy company.*

- *For questions 6–10, decide which place (A–H) is best suited to the needs on the opposite page.*

- *For each question, mark the correct letter (A–H).*

- *Do not use any letter more than once.*

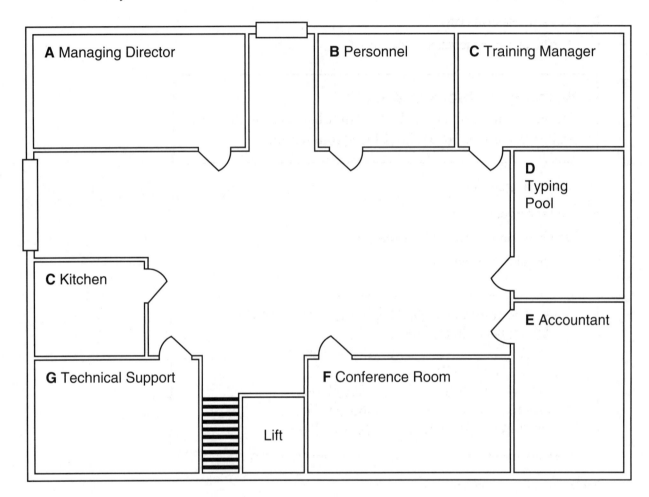

6   There has been an electrical problem and all the computers are down.

7   You have written a draft report on your lap-top and now you want it checked and printed.

8   The company has invited a group of specialists to the office for a one-day meeting.

9   You have been asked to check if there will be enough coffee, tea, sugar, soft drinks, etc, for refreshments at the conference.

10   You need to get copies of the CVs of three members of staff.

EXAM INFORMATION

Part Two of the reading test contains an item which has eight parts to it. It might be:

- 8 rooms or sections of an office building
- 8 courses or classes at a training establishment
- 8 chapters of a book
- 8 entries in a directory, catalogue or guide
- 8 staff positions in an organisation diagram
- 8 departments of a shop, company, etc.

In the test there are five statements which you have to match the eight parts in the item. This part of the test is to see how carefully you read to match each statement to the correct part of the item.

A DETAILED STUDY

1   Before you do the test, look at the office plan and answer these questions.

   Who in a company is usually responsible for:

   1   producing documents, letters, etc?

   2   making policy decisions?

   3   maintaining and repairing office equipment?

   4   dealing with staff problems, such as illness, absenteeism, etc?

   5   dealing with the company's financial affairs?

   6   helping staff to learn new skills and knowledge?

2   Look at sentences **6–10** on page 41 then read the sentences below and write *True* or *False*.

   1   *The computers are down* means the computers are all on the floor.

   2   A draft report needs to be checked and revised before it is ready.

   3   Specialists are experts in a particular subject.

   4   Refreshments include such things as taking a shower or washing your hands.

   5   A CV tells you about a person's qualifications and work experience.

Now answer questions 6–10 in Part Two of the reading test on page 41.

PART THREE

Questions 11–15

- *Look at the chart below. It shows the record of injuries in an industrial company during the eight years 1994–2001.*

- *Which year in the chart does each sentence (11–15) on the opposite page describe?*

- *For each sentence, mark one letter (A–H).*

- *Do not use any letter more than once.*

Injury Record

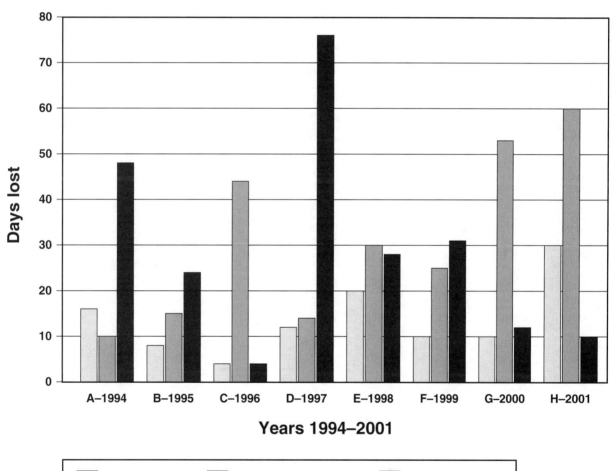

11   There was a record number of injuries but only a slight increase in the amount of time lost.

12   Time lost was up on previous years with a record amount of time required for medical treatment.

13   There were very few serious injuries but many minor injuries, which meant that medical treatment was up 300% on the previous year.

14   The number of serious injuries was well down on the previous year but the need for medical treatment doubled.

15   Time lost through injury was half that of the previous year as was the number of serious injuries.

Before you check your answers, go to page 45.

EXAM INFORMATION

In Part Three of the reading test, information is presented in graphic form. It might be a chart, a histogram, a graph or a table.

There are always eight pieces of information showing trends. These may describe how things:

- get bigger or smaller
- become more or become less
- increase or decrease
- remain steady (stay the same)
- grow or decline
- expand or reduce.

To describe a trend, we **compare** (make comparisons). For example:

- comparing the second quarter with the first (previous) quarter
- comparing this month with all the previous or all the following months

The subjects of the graphic include:

- financial information: sales figures, share prices, income, expenditure, etc
- regular events: industrial accidents, absenteeism, enquiries, etc
- results: of surveys, advertising campaigns, etc.

The time scale may be daily, weekly monthly, quarterly or annually.

The test has five statements which you have to match to the eight parts in the graphic.

This part of the test is checking to see how carefully you can interpret a graphic.

A DETAILED STUDY

1   Look at these phrases which can be used to describe trends. Write **B** (getting better), **W** (getting worse) or **S** (staying the same) next to each phrase:

1	a disastrous fall in business	12	remained steady
2	a peak in July	13	fell in the second half
3	a slight dip	14	roughly the same
4	a slight increase	15	picked up well
5	began to fall off	16	reached an amazing peak
6	continued to grow steadily	17	sales were at record levels
7	did equally well	18	slightly ahead
8	doubled	19	starting and finishing badly
9	falling steadily	20	tailed off in the last quarter
10	fell continuously	21	remained low all year
11	gradually picked up	22	down on the previous year

2   Study the graphic in this test on page 43 and try to identify which year these statements refer to.

1   There were more serious injuries in this year than in any other.

2   The year when least time was lost.

3   Second highest year for time spent on medical treatment.

4   This was the year when most time was lost.

5   A record low for time spent on medical treatment.

Now check your answers to Part Three of the reading test.

PART FOUR

Questions 16–22

- *Read the following minutes of a meeting.*

- *Are the sentences 16–22 on the opposite page right or wrong? If there is not enough information to answer 'Right' or 'Wrong', choose 'Doesn't Say'.*

- *For each sentence, mark one letter (A, B or C).*

DeBolt Group of Companies

Minutes of Training Managers' Meeting

Tuesday, 10 November 2004 at Group Head Office

Present

5   S Rogers (Group Chairman), M Allen, G Bowyer, T Chipp (part), H Douglas, R Emery, R Fairchild

Apologies for absence

P Grope (on a training course), L Hart (ill), and W Ibsley (on maternity leave)

Agenda: Foreign Language Training

The Group Chairman proposed that every employee should learn two foreign languages, of
10   which one should be either Portuguese or Spanish.

Decisions taken

It was agreed that:

- each training manager should find out if any employees already had a knowledge of these or other foreign languages.

15 - the best way to provide the training is to run courses giving 4 hours of tuition per week, timing to be decided.

- each company in the Group should be responsible for finding suitable materials and local providers of language training.

- M Allen, H Douglas and R Fairchild will form a working group to draft a <u>Foreign Language</u>
20   <u>Training Policy Document</u>.

The draft Policy Document will be presented at the next Training Managers' Meeting.

16   W Ibsley was too ill to attend the meeting.

A   Right   **B**   Wrong   **C**   Doesn't say

17   The group chairman wants everyone to learn Portuguese and Spanish.

A   Right   **B**   Wrong   **C**   Doesn't say

18   Some employees already know a foreign language.

A   Right   **B**   Wrong   **C**   Doesn't say

19   The working group will meet regularly to review the draft.

A   Right   **B**   Wrong   **C**   Doesn't say

20   All the members of the Policy Document Working Group were present at this meeting.

A   Right   **B**   Wrong   **C**   Doesn't say

21   The language courses will take place on company premises.

A   Right   **B**   Wrong   **C**   Doesn't say

22   Each company will set up its own language training programme.

A   Right   **B**   Wrong   **C**   Doesn't say

PART FIVE

Questions 23–28

- *Read the text below about the financier Muriel Siebert.*

- *For each question 23–28 on the opposite page, choose the correct answer.*

- *Mark one letter (A, B or C).*

The First Woman of Finance

Muriel Siebert was the first woman to have a seat on the New York Stock Exchange, and the first to head one of its member firms, Muriel Siebert & Co. She took leave in 1977 to serve as the first woman Superintendent of Banking for the State of New York. She often appears on talk shows, telling industry to make better use of women: 'Women executives can be a strong competitive force against other countries that still only employ males in executive positions.'

Her favourite word is 'risk'. She says: 'The men at the top of industry and government should risk sharing leadership with women. In these fast-changing times we need different viewpoints and experiences. The real risk lies in continuing to do things the way they've always been done.'

Her best-known 'risk' was in 1967 when she applied to become the first woman member of the Stock Exchange. Many men on Wall Street were openly against her application. She was turned down by nine of the first ten men she asked to sponsor her application. Before considering her for membership, the Stock Exchange set a new condition: she needed a letter from a bank saying they would lend her $300,000 of the $445,000 seat price. But banks would not lend her the money until the Stock Exchange agreed to admit her! The problem was finally solved and she was elected to membership in December 1967. In December 1997 she celebrated her thirtieth anniversary by ringing the closing bell.

Her next career move was to the post of Superintendent of New York State's Banking Department. In the 1970s, banks were facing many difficulties. Interest rates climbed steeply and bank failures became common everywhere. Siebert acted quickly to prevent bankruptcies in New York State. She forced banks to merge, persuading stronger institutions to help weaker ones, and demanded tough action, such as forcing one bank president to cut his salary in half.

During this period, she had placed her company in a blind trust run by her employees, that is, a trust which managed a company for her while she held public office. It was a costly mistake: she discovered that three employees had left taking her customer lists with them. She rebuilt the company, and rejected offers to buy her company because: 'As the only woman owner of a Stock Exchange firm I feel an obligation to finish the job I started.'

23   Muriel Siebert was the first woman to

    A   own her own company.

    B   run a New York bank.

    C   join the Stock Exchange.

24   According to Siebert, if more women get into senior positions, it will

    A   show that women are just as good as men.

    B   make American companies more competitive.

    C   encourage American companies to take risks.

25   The worst risk, according to Siebert, is to

    A   do nothing.

    B   change things too quickly.

    C   employ more men than women.

26   What did Siebert need to do in order to enter the Stock Exchange?

    A   find a sponsor and get a bank loan.

    B   send the completed application form to her bank.

    C   get a seat and ring the closing bell.

27   In the late seventies, one problem faced by companies and financial institutions was that

    A   wages were too high.

    B   banks often refused to lend money.

    C   interest rates kept going up and up.

28   What went wrong with her firm while it was in a blind trust?

    A   It lost most of its customers.

    B   Nobody would buy it.

    C   She still had to finish the job she had started.

PART SIX

Questions 29–40

- *Read the article below about mission statements.*

- *Choose the correct word to fill each gap, from **A, B** or **C** on the opposite page.*

- *For each question **29–40**, mark one letter (**A, B** or **C**).*

Mission Statements:
saying what your company's aims are

Mission statements are not easy to write. Most are too simple, or they are

(29) .... long that nobody takes **(30)** .... notice of them.

When I was advising a large company, I suggested **(31)** .... the chairman

that it ought to have a mission statement. He replied, 'I don't want

(32) ....!' When I asked him why not, he said that it would

(33) .... nothing for the business.

A good mission statement **(34)** .... to be clear, and to say in a few words

(35) .... a company is trying to do. It should be **(36)** .... in all the

company's documents. Tesco, a British supermarket chain, describes

(37) .... mission as follows: 'To earn the lifelong loyalty of Tesco's

customers.'

It **(38)** .... a wonderful example of a mission statement: short and easy to

remember. We know it has worked

(39) .... the company is now the biggest supermarket retailer **(40)** ....

Britain.

29 **A** very   **B** too   **C** so

30 **A** any   **B** the   **C** a

31 **A** to   **B** about   **C** for

32 **A** it   **B** one   **C** them

33 **A** make   **B** do   **C** have

34 **A** need   **B** needs   **C** needed

35 **A** what   **B** that   **C** which

36 **A** showed   **B** showing   **C** shown

37 **A** their   **B** her   **C** its

38 **A** is   **B** has   **C** does

39 **A** although   **B** while   **C** because

40 **A** in   **B** of   **C** from

PART SEVEN
Questions 41–45

- *Read the note and the attached job details below.*

- *Complete the form on the opposite page.*

- *Write a word or phrase (in CAPITAL LETTERS) or a number on lines 41–45.*

Ali

I spoke to Michael Byers (Pettivale Garden Supplies) re non-payment of our Invoice #RT2124. He says they received RT2123 twice, but not RT2124! Can you issue a fresh invoice, please (JOB details attached). I think we should ask for payment within five days, don't you? And make sure it goes direct to him, OK?

Lakmi

JOB #555	**Date:** 02.02.04
Item:	Repairs to VGS delivery van
Parts:	£144.00
Labour:	£350.00
Total:	£494.00
Signed:	JKL

INVOICE TO:

Company: (41) ....

Twentypence Road

Verwood BH12 6TT

Invoice number (re-issue):   (42) ....

For the attention of: (43) ....

Details of service provided: (44) ....

Amount due: (45) ....

Terms of payment: *5 working days from*

receipt of invoice

WRITING

PART ONE

Question 46

- *You are scheduled to visit several clients around the country and your own car is not available.*

- *Write a **memo** to John Oates, the head of the company motor pool:*

  - *explaining your problem*

  - *requesting a car from the company motor pool*

  - *saying what kind of car you would like and when you will need it.*

- *Write **30–40** words.*

MEMO

To: John Oates
From:
Date:
Re: **Request for company car**

....

....

....

....

....

....

....

....

PART TWO
Question 47

- *Read this letter of complaint from a customer.*

Dear Sir or Madam

Our Order Number 19445

On 5 June, we ordered ten packs of Document Wallets from your Catalogue (Page 79) as follows:

Cat no	Colour	Qty
334 151	blue	6
334 219	green	2
334 250	yellow	2

When we received this order, we found that you had sent us ten packs of red (Cat no 334 243) instead. We noticed that the delivery note enclosed with the order was made out to a different firm, which might explain the error.

We look forward to receiving an explanation of this mistake.

Yours faithfully

A. Poilue

Annette Poilue
Office Manager

- *Write a **letter** to Ms Poilue:*

  - *thanking her for her letter*

  - *apologizing for the error*

  - *explaining what happened*

  - *saying what you are going to do about it.*

- *Write **60–80** words.*

- *Do not include postal addresses.*

Before you write your letter, go to page 56.

EXAM INFORMATION

In Part Two of the writing test, you have to read a text and reply to it. The text might be the form of a letter, a fax message, a note or an email.

The sender might be:

- a customer: asking for help or making a complaint
- a colleague: asking you to do something, or reporting on company matters
- a company: telling you about its product or service.

You are asked to reply to the incoming text with a letter, fax or email of about 60–80 words. Your reply needs to contain three or four points, such as:

A	giving information	F	inviting someone
B	asking for information	G	accepting an invitation
C	confirming an arrangement or order	H	thanking someone for something
D	asking for confirmation	I	offering an explanation
E	making a reservation	J	asking for an explanation

Look at the following phrases and say which of the categories (**A–J**) each one belongs to.

1   ... there is some confusion as to dates, so will you please confirm ...

2   It was very good of you to display our leaflets on your stand at the exhibition ...

3   Can you let us know the cost of ...

4   Can you please tell us why you did not inform us ...

5   Ms Bunce is pleased to accept your kind invitation to ...

6   ... we would like to book the conference hall ...

7   Please let me know when ...

8   The error was probably the result of a misunderstanding ...

9   ... we would be delighted to see you at our office ...

10   ... we can confirm that ...

A DETAILED STUDY

Read this model answer to Question 47.

1   Has the writer has covered all the points? If not, make a note of any that were missed.

2   Find and correct seven mistakes in this letter: two in spelling and five in grammar.

> Dear Ms Poilue
> I have looked into the matter and can confirmed that, as you suspected, we sent you someone else order by mistake. Your correct order will be send to you today by Express Delivery. We would like you to acept the goods free of charge. We should also like you to keeping the 10 packs of red wallets with our compliments.
> We want to assure you that we do everything we can to aviod such mistakes in future.
> Yours sincerely

(79 words)

Now write your own answer to question 47 in Part Two of the writing test. Remember to check for grammar and spelling mistakes.

LISTENING 40 minutes

PART ONE

Questions 1–8

- *For questions 1–8 you will hear eight short recordings.*

- *For each question, mark one letter (A, B or C) for the most suitable picture or phrase.*

Example:

What did the sign say?

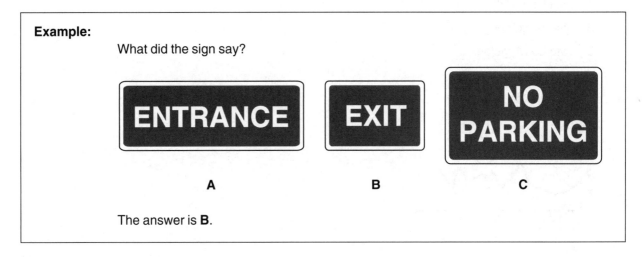

A   B   C

The answer is **B**.

1 When was the stationery ordered?

    A Monday

    B Thursday

    C Friday

2 Who did Chris Sharp used to work for?

    A the government

    B J P Engineering

    C Ashlings

3 What is the company introducing next year?

  A children's wear

  B food products

  C perfume and toiletries

4 Which is the cheapest flight to Sydney?

  A via New York

  B via Hong Kong

  C via Los Angeles

5 Which is the correct chart?

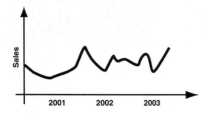

A

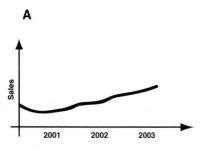

B

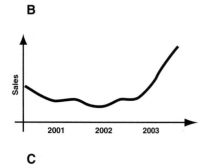

C

6 How will the delegates get to the conference centre?

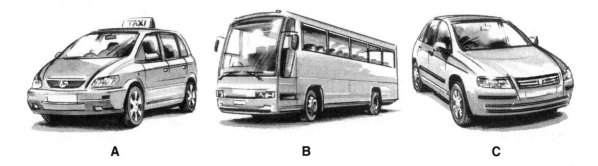

A   B   C

7 Where did the man leave his notes for the meeting?

A   B   C

8 How many chairs are needed for the meeting?

A   B   C

PART TWO
Questions 9–15

- *Look at the notes below.*

- *Some information is missing.*

- *You will hear a man talking to a woman about the additional resources he needs for a project.*

- *For each question 9–15, fill in the missing information in the numbered space using a **time**, **numbers** or **letters**.*

POTTER PROJECT: STAGE TWO
Additional Costs

Additional staff requirements:

(9) .... **programmers** @ total cost of (10) $ ....

Project manager   @ total cost of (11) $ ....

IT requirements:

(12) .... PCs

1 scanner

Other:

(13) .... **photocopier** @ total cost: (14) $ ....

Budget increase of approx. (15) ....

Before you complete the gaps 9–15, go to page 61.

EXAM INFORMATION

In Part Two of the listening test you will hear a short conversation between two people or a monologue. The recording will last about one and a half minutes and you will be tested on your ability to listen for factual information. On your question paper there will be a form, a table, a chart or a set of notes with seven gaps. Your task is to fill in the missing information which may be a date, a price, a percentage or figures.

A DETAILED STUDY

1   Before you listen to Part Two, read the instructions carefully. What **two** things do the instructions tell you about what you are going to hear?

    1   There will be _____ people speaking.

    2   They will be talking about a _____ .

2   Now read the notes and decide for each of the gaps **9–15** if you need a **number** or a **price.**

    (9) ____*number*____

    (10) _____

    (11) _____

    (12) _____

    (13) _____

    (14) ____*price*____

    (15) _____

3   Listen to the recording once only and write down any number or price you hear in the order in which you hear them. There are twelve altogether. We have done some of them for you.

    1   ___*4*___

    2   _____

    3   _____

    4   _____

    5   _____

    6   *$5,000*

    7   _____

    8   _____

    9   ___*3*___

    10   _____

    11   _____

    12   _____

Now you are ready to listen to Part Two of the listening test again and fill in the missing information in gaps 9–15.

PART THREE
Questions 16–22

- *Look at the notes below.*

- *Some information is missing.*

- *You will hear the chief executive of a chain of retail clothes stores talking to the shareholders about the company's activities during the year.*

- *For each question **16–22**, fill in the missing information in the numbered space using **one** or **two** words.*

The Good Clothes Company

Introduction: What went wrong?
                   (refer to date two years ago: **(16)** ....)

Customers' opinions
- clothes: **(17)** ....
- stores: badly-designed
- prices: too high

What did we try?
- mail-shot to our credit card customers
- **(18)** .... with customers visiting our stores
- detailed survey of customers' buying habits

What did we find out?
Customers wanted:
- better lighting and plenty of **(19)** .... in the stores
- good displays
- clothes available in all **(20)** ....
- high quality at the right price.

What changes did we make?
- put in automatic **(21)** ....
- improved the lighting
- arranged better displays
- maintained quality
- reduced **(22)** ....
- introduced new range of clothes

Before you complete the gaps 16–22, go to page 63.

EXAM INFORMATION

In Part Three of the listening test you will hear one person speaking. Usually they are giving a speech or a talk about something. The aim of this part of the test is to test your ability to listen for specific details. On the question paper will be a set of notes with gaps. Your task is to fill in the missing information with one or two words.

A DETAILED STUDY

1   Before you listen to Part Three, read the instructions carefully. What **three** things do the instructions tell you about what you are going to hoar?

    1   The person who is speaking is the _____ of a chain of _____ .

    2   She is making a speech to the _____ .

    3   The speech is about the activities of the _____.

2   Now read the notes she has made for her speech and decide what four areas she is going to talk about.

    1   What went _____?

    2   What did we _____?

    3   What _____?

    4   _____?

3   Look at each numbered gap and decide what sort of word or words you are looking for.

    Example: *Question 17*   *adjective?*

                (the word must be something about the sort of clothes they were selling)

Now you are ready to listen Part Three of the listening test again and fill in the missing information in gaps 16–22.

PART FOUR
Questions 23–30

- *You will hear a radio interview with Philippe Salenbier, the director of Vaporette International.*

- *For each question 23–30, mark one letter (A, B or C) for the correct answer.*

23 The interviewer thinks Philippe Salenbier does not look like an expert in aerosols because he is

    A   wearing glasses.

    B   too young for the job.

    C   dressed too smartly.

24 What is Philippe's main aim?

    A   to make his company larger

    B   to sell direct to supermarkets

    C   to change the shape of aerosols

25 What makes his company attractive to work for?

    A   its location

    B   high salaries

    C   company cars

26 What is the company going to do to improve their skills shortage?

    A   develop and train staff already working for them

    B   employ some skilled staff on temporary contracts

    C   offer financial help for people to move to the area

27 What is Philippe pleased about?

    A the variety of Vaporette products on the shelves

    B the increase in sales and annual turnover

    C the collapse of a rival aerosol company

28 What has had most influence on the cost of aerosols?

    A finding new markets to sell to in the Far East

    B the cost of some ingredients in Europe

    C the demands of retailers to keep prices low

29 How does the company try to avoid disappointing customers?

    A It does not charge for delivery.

    B It only uses top quality ingredients.

    C It keeps extra stocks of products.

30 How will the company improve its sales in quiet periods?

    A reduce prices after the Christmas period

    B develop aerosols for the home and garden

    C offer reductions on certain products

SPEAKING   12 minutes

PART ONE (ABOUT 2 MINUTES)

In this part of the test the examiner (interlocutor) will ask each of you some questions about where you work or study, where you live or what you do in your free time. Here are some sample questions:

- Are you a student or do you have a job?
- What are you studying?
- What do you enjoy most about being a student?
- Where would you like to study abroad?
- Why is that?
- Do you like playing/watching sport?
- How often do you play/watch this sport?

PART TWO (ABOUT 5 MINUTES)

In this part of the test you are asked to give a 'mini presentation'. You have a choice of topic such as those below and you have one minute to prepare what you are going to say. After you have spoken, the examiner will ask your partner to say something about what you have said. After you have listened to your partner's presentation, the examiner will ask you to say something about what your partner has said.

Prompt Card (a)   *(Given to Candidate A, and a copy to Candidate B)*

> **A: WHAT IS IMPORTANT WHEN ...?**
>
> **Choosing a conference site**
>
> - Location
> - Facilities
> - Cost

Prompt Card (b)   *(Given to Candidate B, and a copy to Candidate A)*

> **B: WHAT IS IMPORTANT WHEN ...?**
>
> **Marketing a new product**
>
> - Advertising
> - Delivery
> - Quality

Now go to pages 67–68.

EXAM INFORMATION

In Part Two of the speaking test you will be asked to speak for about one minute on a business topic. This is called a 'mini-presentation'. You will be able to choose from two topics. Each topic is written on a card with three points about it. You can talk about some or all of these points. Once you have chosen your topic, you have one minute to prepare. You need to speak for at least 45 seconds.

After each of you has finished speaking, the interlocutor will ask the other candidate(s) a question about what you have been talking about.

This part of the test lasts for about five minutes.

The aim of this part of the test is to see how well you present some basic ideas and how you structure what you are going to say.

A DETAILED STUDY

1   Look at the topic card below read the sentences **A–I**. Write each letter, **A–I**, under the correct headings in the table.

> ### A: WHAT IS IMPORTANT WHEN ... ?
>
> **Choosing a conference site**
>
> - Location
> - Facilities
> - Cost

A   Check there is a room big enough for everyone attending.

B   It's important for people to get there easily.

C   Usually the delegates will pay to come.

D   There must be enough accommodation for everyone.

E   Find out how much they are going to charge.

F   It's a good idea if it's situated near a train station or an airport.

G   They should be able to provide meals and refreshments.

H   There needs to be a budget and then you must stick to it.

I   A hotel is probably a good place to choose.

Location	Facilities	Cost B
B		

2   Look at the topic card below and complete each sentence using one of the phrases **A–F**.

B: WHAT IS IMPORTANT WHEN … ?

Marketing a new product

- Advertising

- Quality

- Delivery

Advertising

1   The first thing to do is …

2   I think it's important to remember …

3   It's also a good idea to consider …

Quality

1   Before sending a product out …

2   It's easier to sell if …

3   Deal with any problems about quality …

A   you know a lot about your product.

B   that a good product will almost sell itself.

C   as soon as you know about them.

D   decide what sort of advertising is appropriate.

E   check that it is complete.

F   what sort of people will buy your product.

3   Complete each of these sentences using the words in brackets.

Delivery

1   Make sure … (sufficient stocks)

2   Don't forget … (pack carefully)

3   It's vital … (despatch dates)

Now look again at the prompt cards in Part Two of the speaking test.

PART THREE (ABOUT 5 MINUTES)

The examiner will describe a situation to you and give you a few sentences to help you. You have 30 seconds to look at the prompt card and two minutes to discuss the situation. The examiner will then ask you some more questions about the situation.

Here is the situation:

You have been asked to select three people to interview for a post in your company. Talk together for about two minutes about the things you think are important about the new person. Decide which three things are the most important.

Here are some ideas to help you:

- Experience in a similar job
- Educational qualifications
- Skills
- Age
- Interests and hobbies
- Reasons for wanting the job

TEST THREE

READING AND WRITING 1 hour 30 minutes

PART ONE

Questions 1–5

- *Look at questions **1–5**.*

- *In each question, which sentence is correct?*

- *For each question, mark one letter (**A, B** or **C**).*

Example:

0 | Susan's arriving at 8.45pm tomorrow. Can you collect her from the station?

Susan arrives at

A quarter to eight tomorrow morning.

B quarter to nine tomorrow evening.

C quarter to nine tomorrow morning.

The correct answer is **B**, so mark your answer sheet like this:

1

Company staff are reminded that no documents may be taken from the filing room without the permission of the librarian.

A You must ask the librarian if you want to take documents out of the filing room.

B No one is allowed to take documents out of the filing room.

C The librarian needs permission to take documents out of the filing room.

2

STANWAY FERRIES CAR STORAGE

Situated near the ferry terminal
£6.50 per day for first 15 days, then £3.00 per day
Car cleaning service available
Reservations: Tel   09932 45000
                    Email   stanway@timenet.co.uk
Booking online www.stanway.com/reservations

This company allows people to

A   get a free ride to the terminal.

B   have their car serviced.

C   leave their car close to the terminal.

3

PARKING RESERVED FOR STAFF ONLY
VISITORS USE PUBLIC CAR PARK IN BEWICK ROAD
(LEFT AT THE END OF THE BUILDING)

Visitors should park their cars

A   at the end of the building.

B   in Bewick Road.

C   behind the building.

4

Marissa
Robin from Robin's Cafe phoned re your call. They say they never received Invoice ER213. Can you get back to him asap.
Carmina.

What is Robin's problem regarding Invoice ER213?

A   He has no record of it.

B   His company is late sending it.

C   He needs to talk to Carmina about it.

5

10% discount if you pay your bill within 30 days of receipt of goods.

To get the discount, you must

A   receive the goods within thirty days.

B   deliver the goods within thirty days.

C   pay for the goods within thirty days.

PART TWO

Questions 6–10

- Look at the box files on this shelf. They are in the office of the woman who produces the monthly company newsletter.

- For questions **6–10** on the opposite page, decide which file (**A–H**) she needs to consult.

- Do not use any letter more than once.

6 She needs to get in touch with all the company's distributors in South America.

7 She has a pile of letters that she needs to file.

8 She wants to compare the company's latest product with similar products on the market.

9 She wants to check an article from an old newsletter.

10 She is writing an article about a supplier from whom her company buys spare parts.

PART THREE

Questions 11–15

- *Look at the graphs below. They show the response to TV and magazine advertisements for eight different holidays over a four-month period.*

- *Which chart does each sentence (11–15) on the opposite page describe?*

- *For each sentence, mark one letter (A–H).*

- *Do not use any letter more than once.*

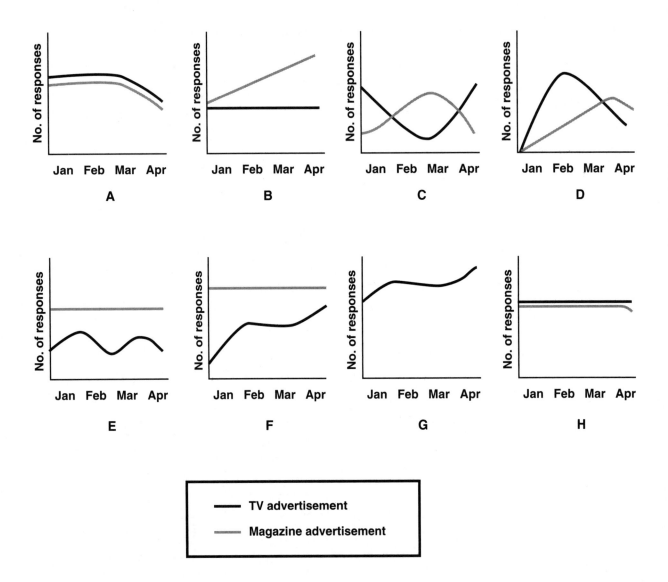

11   Responses to the TV advertisement for this holiday remained steady over the four months, while responses to the magazine advertisement continued to grow steadily.

12   The magazine advertisement for this holiday did much better than the TV advertisement throughout, although the TV advertisement gradually picked up well, particularly in April.

13   The advertisements for this holiday did equally well, but responses to the magazine advertisement began to fall off towards the end of the period.

14   Interest in this holiday varied a lot over the four-month period with the magazine advertisement starting and finishing badly, almost the opposite of the TV advertisement's performance.

15   Both media did well, with the TV advertisement slightly ahead of the magazine advertisement, although both tailed off in April.

PART FOUR

Questions 16–22

- *Read the following job advertisement.*

- *Are the sentences **16–22** on the opposite page right or wrong? If there is not enough information to answer 'Right' or 'Wrong', choose 'Doesn't say'.*

- *For each sentence **16–22**, mark one letter (**A**, **B** or **C**).*

Job Vacancy
Administrator for our
Volunteer Programme

We need a well-motivated administrator for our busy central office at our
national headquarters. The person appointed will play an important part
in providing administrative support services to the Programme Manager.

The Administrator's duties will include co-ordinating staff recruitment
and appointment procedures nationwide. You will need to have excellent
secretarial, organizational and communication skills plus an ability to
meet deadlines promptly and efficiently. A knowledge of the latest
versions of Word and Wordperfect is essential. You must also be able to
read spreadsheets produced in QuattroPro or Excel.

For a job description and an application form (please do not send CVs at
this stage), call our 24-hour answerphone on 0208 343 8000. Or you can
email us on VProg@nethere.com, marked for the attention of Melanie
Slim, and giving reference VP3420. Closing date for applications is 7th
March. Interviews will take place at our national HQ on 18th March.

16   The administrator will have his/her own office at national headquarters.

    A   Right   **B**   Wrong   **C**   Doesn't say

17   The administrator's duties include appointing new staff.

    A   Right   **B**   Wrong   **C**   Doesn't say

18   The successful applicant will be able to work without supervision.

    A   Right   **B**   Wrong   **C**   Doesn't say

19   Applicants should include their CVs when they send for the application form.

    A   Right   **B**   Wrong   **C**   Doesn't say

20   Applicants can phone for details and a form at any time.

    A   Right   **B**   Wrong   **C**   Doesn't say

21   Applications must be in by 7th March at the latest.

    A   Right   **B**   Wrong   **C**   Doesn't say

22   Candidates will be interviewed by Melanie Slim.

    A   Right   **B**   Wrong   **C**   Doesn't say

PART FIVE

Questions 23–28

Before you read the text, go to question 1 on page 80.

- *Read the text below about handling complaints.*

- *For each question 23–28 on the opposite page, choose the correct answer.*

- *Mark one letter (A, B or C).*

Handling Complaints

Big companies have a special department to deal with customer complaints.
Complaints can often be handled 'on the spot', that is, at the time of
purchase. If it is just a matter of changing or exchanging goods, the sales
5 assistant can deal with it. Some problems are more complicated: damaged
goods, a request for a refund or a complaint about staff rudeness. At this
point a Supervisor or someone from Customer Services is usually called in.
But if the matter still cannot be solved, which is usually because the
customer refuses to listen or to accept the offered solution, it is referred to
10 someone higher up, such as the Store Manager. Or, if the store is part of a
national chain, the complaint will be dealt with by Head Office.

The policy of the big chain stores is: 'Accept that things can go wrong and
put them right.' They sell a billion items a year and they know that not all
their goods are going to be perfect. They accept, therefore, that most (if not
15 all) customer complaints are justified.

It's all about customer loyalty. What if a store refuses to listen to a customer's
complaint (whether justified or unjustified)? The store then has an unhappy
customer, but has done nothing to make that customer happy again. That
customer will not come back. But if the store listens politely, checks the
20 problem, and then offers a replacement or a refund, with an apology if
needed, the customer will remain loyal.

A recent survey shows that customer complaints are increasing. The
commonest complaint is about staff who are unhelpful, usually because they
know little about the product they are selling. The second thing that makes
25 customers angry is having to wait too long to be served. Recently, many
retailers have cut running costs by employing fewer staff, so there simply
aren't enough sales assistants or staff at the checkout desks.

It is not clear why complaints are on the increase. Maybe standards of service
are going down, but the more likely explanation is that people are readier to
30 complain nowadays. Citizens' Charters, telling people what they can expect
and what to do if they are dissatisfied, have produced a generation of
customers who know their rights and not afraid to demand them.

23   What can be offered on the spot if a customer complains?

    A   a full refund of the purchase price

    B   a replacement of the original item

    C   an apology for impolite behaviour

24   A complaint would be referred to the Store Manager or Head Office when

    A   a customer remains dissatisfied.

    B   a customer has been overcharged.

    C   a customer has been rude to staff.

25   The big chain stores accept a customer's complaint because

    A   they accept that there will always be some damaged or faulty goods.

    B   they believe 'the customer is always right'.

    C   only a small percentage of imperfect goods are returned.

26   According to the writer, a store can keep its customers happy by

    A   agreeing with them whether they are right or wrong.

    B   referring them to Head Office in serious cases.

    C   always taking notice of their complaints.

27   According to the writer, why does it often take so long to get served?

    A   Staff don't know enough to answer customers' questions.

    B   There are not enough checkout desks in most stores.

    C   Stores have reduced the number of sales staff.

28   The writer believes there are more customer complaints these days because

    A   people are more aware of their rights than they used to be.

    B   young people are more likely to complain than older people.

    C   stores don't listen to what their customers are telling them.

Before you check your answers, go to question 2 on page 80.

EXAM INFORMATION

Part Five of the reading test has a long reading text followed by six multiple-choice questions. The questions (**23–28**) each have three options. You have to choose the option which matches the information in the text.

This part tests how carefully you read the text, and how well you are able to match the correct option to information in the text.

A DETAILED STUDY

1   This activity will help you to think about the important points in the text. Before you read the text, look at the statements below and decide which are true and which are false.

   1   Big companies usually have a department to deal with complaints.

   2   Difficult customers are dealt with on the spot.

   3   The store manager must authorize change or exchange of goods.

   4   If you ignore a customer's complaint, you are likely to lose that customer.

   5   Customers complain more than they used to.

   6   The biggest complaint is about sales staff being impolite.

   7   Customers get upset if they have to wait a long time to get served.

   8   Citizens' Charters tell people what their rights are.

Now read the text and answer questions 23–28 in Part Five of the reading test.

2   The questions below will help you understand the text better and make sure you choose the correct options for questions **23–28**.

   23   What does *on the spot* mean? Who is the person on the spot who deals with the customer? (lines 3–5).

   24   What examples of more 'complicated' cases are listed in the text? (lines 5–6)

   25   What are *chain stores* and what is usually their policy on complaints? (lines 12–15)

   26   What is the best way to keep a customer's loyalty? (line 16, and lines 19–21)

   27   In what way are staff often 'unhelpful'? (lines 23–24)

   28   What has made customers more aware of their rights and encouraged them to complain more? (lines 30–32)

Now check your answers to Part Five of the reading test.

PART SIX
Questions 29–40

- *Read the magazine article about business English.*

- *Choose the correct word to fill each gap, from **A**, **B** or **C** below.*

- *For each question **29–40**, mark one letter (**A**, **B** or **C**).*

Business English

English is becoming an international business language. This is **(29)** .... more and more companies are providing English language training for **(30)** .... employees. It can be very expensive, so companies should find out **(31)** .... really needs English and for what purpose. In a tourist hotel, **(32)** .... example, the manager **(33)** .... not need to use English much, except to **(34)** .... with complaints or to talk to important business contacts. The waiters, **(35)** .... the other hand, use English all the time. A manager and a waiter need different kinds of

English, so the training **(36)** .... gets will also be very different. Then, some employees only **(37)** .... a reading knowledge of English, so it would be a waste of money to train **(38)** .... employees in conversational skills.

But companies should also **(39)** .... into account the wishes of the employees themselves. Many people want to learn English, not just for their present job, **(40)** .... because they see it as a passport to a better job in the future.

29	**A** why	**B** that	**C** because
30	**A** her	**B** its	**C** their
31	**A** which	**B** who	**C** what
32	**A** by	**B** to	**C** for
33	**A** must	**B** can	**C** may
34	**A** deal	**B** answer	**C** handle
35	**A** with	**B** in	**C** on
36	**A** either	**B** every	**C** each
37	**A** needed	**B** need	**C** needs
38	**A** same	**B** like	**C** such
39	**A** take	**B** put	**C** have
40	**A** but	**B** for	**C** so

Before you check your answers, go to page 82.

EXAM INFORMATION

In Part Six of the reading test there is a short reading text with ten gaps. For each gap, there are three options. You have to choose the option which fits the meaning of the sentence and is also grammatically correct.

Part Six tests:

- prepositions: *of, to, with*, etc
- pronouns: *who, which, whose*, etc
- verb tenses: *is doing, has done, had done*, etc
- modal verbs: *must, can, should, may*, etc
- other grammar points: articles (*the, a*), *some/any, too/very*, etc
- phrasal verbs: *make up, come across*, etc
- fixed expressions: *on the other hand, spend time, go for a walk*, etc
- confusing pairs: *such/so, why/because, then/than, do/make*, etc.

A DETAILED STUDY

1   Read the following sentences and study the way the words in italics are used. Decide which word in italics would best fit the gap in the text on page 81.

29	why	I don't like big towns. That's *why* I live in a country village.
	that	It's not that I dislike towns, it's *that* I dislike noise and dirt.
	because	I live in a country village *because* I don't like big towns.
30	her	This is my sister and this is *her* dog.
	its	The dog spends most of *its* time sleeping.
	their	Dogs spend most of *their* time sleeping.
31	who	Can you tell me *who* has the key to the library?
	which	Can you tell me *which* of the secretaries has the key?
	what	Can you tell me *what* I have to do to get into the library?
33	must	You *must* not be late for the meeting; it's very important.
	can	I *can* not see you now, I am much too busy.
	may	I *may* not come to the meeting; I have so many other things to do.
36	either	You can take *either* road: they both lead into town.
	every	They say that *every* journey begins with the first step.
	each	A boss should know all his employees and treat *each* the same.
37	needed	I was so dirty that I *needed* a bath.
	need	What I *need* now is a glass of water.
	needs	John *needs* to talk less and think more.
38	same	An invoice is not quite the *same* thing as a bill.
	like	An invoice is *like* a bill because they both tell you what you have to pay.
	such	This report is full of spelling mistakes! How do *such* things happen?
40	but	You not only have to write the report, *but* you also have to deliver it.
	and	You have to write the report *and* then deliver it.
	so	You don't have much time, *so* you should get on with it right away.

For tho oorrcct answers, see the Key to Test Three Part Six.

PART SEVEN

Questions 41–45

- *Read the note and the leaflet below.*

- *Complete the form at the bottom of the page.*

- *Write a word or phrase (in CAPITAL LETTERS) or a number on lines 41–45.*

Silvano

Anna, our Canteen Supervisor, wants to change her
supplier from Mammo Foods to a company called
Ottimo. I have spoken to the owner of Ottimo, and will
send a letter today confirming that we wish to open an
account with them. They usually give a 10% discount on
orders over €75.00, but I managed to get us 15%. Let
Anna know that!

Please send a file note to Accounts with the details.

Thanks.

Graziella

Ottimo Bakeries

Prop: Maria Spezzini

Makers of fine bread and cakes
Weddings, banquets, parties

Orders, phone 01023 565715
Other enquiries, call 01023 565704

FILE NOTE: NEW SUPPLIER

Company	**(41)** ....
Contact name	**(42)** ....
Position	**(43)** ....
Phone orders	**(44)** ....
Special arrangements	**(45)** .... *on orders over €75.00*

WRITING

PART ONE

Question 46

- *You work in the Barcelona branch of your company in Spain, and have received an invitation from head office to attend the annual general meeting and dinner in Madrid.*

- *Write an **email** in reply:*

  - *accepting the invitation*

  - *giving your travel details*

  - *requesting help with accommodation.*

- *Write **30–40** words.*

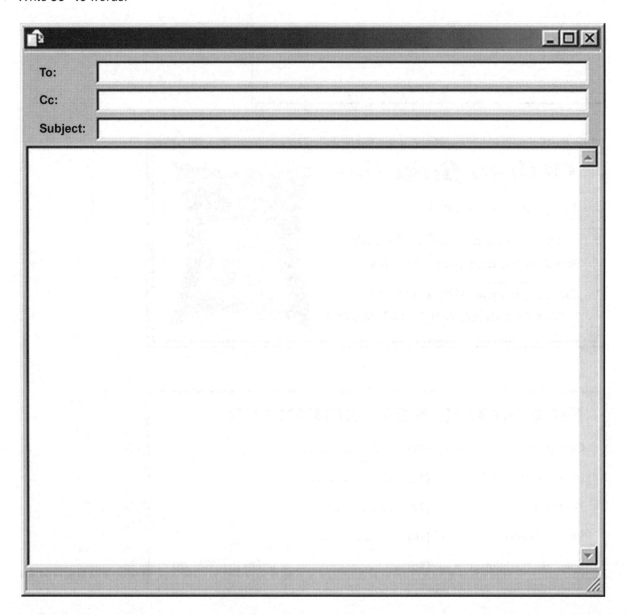

PART TWO
Question 47

- *Read this letter offering you a job.*

---

20 January 2004

Dear ....

Further to your interview for the post of Sales Representative for the South-East Region, we are happy to be able to offer you the job.

As you know, we are launching our new line of cosmetics in April, so we need you to start as soon as possible. Please let us know your earliest start date.

The starting salary as advertised is in the range £40,000-£45,000. We can offer you £42,000, subject to a review after six months when you will have had more experience in the field of cosmetics. Other conditions will be specified in the contract.

We look forward to receiving your acceptance of the post, after which the contract of employment will be sent to you for signature.

Please let me know if you have any questions.

Yours sincerely

M. Starling

Miriam Starling
Chief Executive Officer

- *Write a **letter** to Miriam Starling*

  - *thanking her for her letter*

  - *accepting the post*

  - *giving a reason why you cannot start until May*

  - *saying why you should get a bigger starting salary*

  - *asking for details about 'conditions'.*

- *Write **60–80** words.*

- *Do not include postal addresses.*

Now go to page 86.

FOLLOW UP ACTIVITY

A local electronics company has advertised for a Sales Representative. Two people write to the Personnel Officer, Ms Julie Freeman, asking about the job. Person A is a friend of the Personnel Officer and writes an informal (friendly) letter. Person B does not know Ms Freeman and writes a formal letter.

1   Look at the broken sentences **A–H** below and say which sentences were written by Person A (informal) and which by Person B (formal).

2   Put the sentences into paragraphs and in their correct order.

Dear Anne

Dear Ms Freeman

A
The basic salary you offer seems a bit low, so can you please give me some idea

I would be grateful if you could give me some idea

B
I understand that your company is looking for a Sales Representative.

I hear you're looking for a Sales Rep.

C
May I thank you in advance for your kind attention.

Hope to hear from you soon.

D
I've had lots of sales experience with electronic companies.

My experience includes work in the field of electronics.

E
I'm out of work at the moment, and just can't wait to get another rep's job.

My current status is unemployed, and I am seeking a suitable position in sales.

F
of the level of commission I might expect to earn.

how much I might earn in commission?

G
Therefore, I feel that I am a strong candidate for the post.

So I think I might be just the person you are looking for.

H
Yours

Yours sincerely

LISTENING 40 minutes

PART ONE
Questions 1–8

- *For questions **1–8** you will hear eight short recordings.*

- *For each question, mark one letter (**A**, **B** or **C**) for the most suitable picture or phrase.*

Example:

What did the sign say?

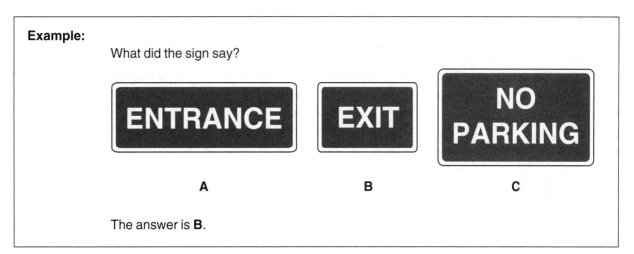

A   B   C

The answer is **B**.

---

1 What do the fruit juice cartons look like at the moment?

A   B   C

2 When will production end?

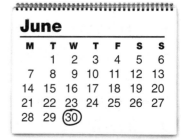

A   B   C

3   Which chart are the men talking about?

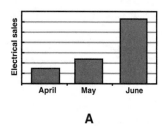

A

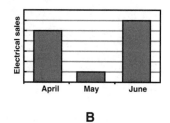

B

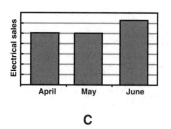

C

4   What message did the man leave?

Can't see you today	*Will call you later today*	*See you tomorrow*
A	**B**	**C**

5   What does the woman want to do?

A   talk to the manager

B   write to the chief executive

C   have a meeting with staff

6   What does the report say is selling best this week?

A

B

C

7   What is the problem in the office today?

A   They have run out of envelopes.

B   The printer needs some more ink.

C   The quality of the labels is poor.

8   Where is the woman meeting Mr Royal?

A   at a hotel

B   at the office

C   at a restaurant

PART TWO

Questions 9–15

- *Look at the form below.*

- *Some information is missing.*

- *You will hear a phone call about an insurance policy.*

- *For each question 9–15, fill in the missing information in the numbered space using a **word** or a **number**.*

PMG PROFESSIONAL INSURANCE

Policy holder: Rebecca **(9)** ....

Policy renewal date: **(10)** ....

Present cover: **(11)** ....

Annual fee: **(12)** ....

Cost per month: **(13)** ....

Cost of cover for £2,000,000:   **(14)** ....

Scheme number: **(15)** ....

PART THREE

Questions 16–22

- *Look at the notes about a business course.*

- *Some information is missing.*

- *You will hear a teacher talking to his students about the course.*

- *For each question 16–22, fill in the missing information in the numbered space using **one** or **two** words.*

Evolve Business Courses

Available dates: (16) ....

Cost includes: (17) ....

Seminars in SWOT analysis and effects of   (18) ....

Guest speakers from the airline sector and   (19) ....

Optional visits to Bank of England and   (20) ....

Successful participants receive   (21) ....

Top student in end of course assessment gets   (22) ....

PART FOUR

Questions 23–30

Before you answer questions 23–30, go to page 93.

- *You will hear a radio interview with Helen James who is a government consultant on employment.*

- *For each question 23–30, mark one letter (A, B or C) for the correct answer.*

23 What has Helen noticed about work patterns?

    A   There is an increase in unemployment.

    B   There are fewer full-time jobs.

    C   More people are being made redundant.

24 Many companies are now offering fewer

    A   permanent jobs.

    B   job contracts.

    C   well-paid jobs.

25 How has part-time work changed now?

    A   It's mainly at weekends and holiday periods.

    B   Most part-time jobs are in shops and restaurants.

    C   In many businesses the majority of staff work part-time.

26 When did Helen work very long hours?

    A   1970s

    B   1980s

    C   1990s

27 Why does she work fewer hours now?

    A   She is self-employed.

    B   She works more efficiently.

    C   She doesn't care so much about her job.

28 What opinion does Helen disagree with?

    A   Part-time workers are not serious about their jobs.

    B   It is not possible for everyone to have a permanent job.

    C   There are many people who do not want full-time jobs.

29 What is the increase in employment since 1995?

    A   5%

    B   18%

    C   22%

30 Which group of people is choosing to work part-time to fund their education?

    A   the over 40s

    B   the over 50s

    C   mothers returning to work

Now go to page 94.

EXAM INFORMATION

In Part Four of the listening test you will hear a longer listening text which may be an interview or discussion between two or more speakers. The recording lasts for about three minutes and you will hear it twice. The aim of this part is to test your ability to pick out specific details and to show a general understanding of the interview or discussion, including any opinions the speakers may express.

There are eight, three-option multiple choice questions in this part of the test. At the end of the listening test you have ten minutes to transfer all your answers on to the answer sheet.
Always take time to read the instructions!

A DETAILED STUDY

1   Before you listen to the recording, read through the questions and their options **A**, **B** and **C**. Which of the statements **1–8** can you say are true **without** listening to the recording?

1   Helen has noticed a change in work patterns.

2   Some companies are offering fewer permanent jobs.

3   There has been a change in part-time work patterns.

4   Helen used to work very long hours.

5   Helen isn't so interested in her job any more.

6   Helen thinks many people don't want to work full-time.

7   There has been an increase in employment since 1995.

8   More mothers are returning to work these days.

2   Listen to the recording once only and answer these general questions about the interview.

1   Who is Helen James?

2   What does Helen research/study?

3   Why can some companies offer high salaries?

4   Are top managers working part-time?

5   What has always been true about the retail industry?

6   Why did Helen work such long hours?

7   What do many people think is a 'real' job?

8   What are many older people doing?

Now you are ready to listen to Part Four of the listening test again and answer questions 23–30.

FURTHER STUDY

In order to help you listen more effectively and deal with multiple choice questions, do this exercise. You will need to read the listening script carefully for this part of the test on page 156.

For each of the multiple choice questions, underline or copy out the parts of the listening script that give you the correct answer.

Example:

23   What has Helen noticed about work patterns?

   A   There is an increase in unemployment.

   <u>**B**</u>   There are fewer full-time jobs.

   C   More people are being made redundant.

More and more people are giving up permanent, full-time jobs.

24   Many companies are now offering fewer

   <u>**A**</u>   permanent jobs.

   B   job contracts.

   C   well-paid jobs.

It is true that many companies no longer offer as many permanent posts as they used to.

SPEAKING 12 minutes

PART ONE   (ABOUT 2 MINUTES)

In this part of the test the examiner (interlocutor) will ask each of you some questions about where you work or study, where you live or what you do in your free time. Here are some sample questions:

- How many hours should people work each week?
- Do you think it is important to work long hours if you want to be successful?
- What other things do you need to do to be successful in your work?
- What do you want to do in the future in your work/studies?
- Why is that?
- What will you be doing in five years' time?

PART TWO   (ABOUT FIVE MINUTES)

In this part of the test you are asked to give a 'mini presentation'. You have a choice of topic such as those below and you have one minute to prepare what you are going to say. After you have spoken, the examiner will ask your partner to say something about what you have said. After you have listened to your partner's presentation, the examiner will ask you to say something about what your partner has said.

Prompt Card (a)   *(Given to Candidate A, and a copy to Candidate B)*

A: WHAT IS IMPORTANT WHEN ...?

Arranging a training day for staff

- Content

- Length of programme

- Venue

Prompt Card (b)   *(Given to Candidate B, and a copy to Candidate A)*

B: WHAT IS IMPORTANT WHEN ...?

Making an appointment

- Date and time

- Length of appointment

- Meeting place

PART THREE (ABOUT 5 MINUTES)

The examiner will describe a situation to you and give you a few sentences to help you. You are asked to discuss the situation with your partner. The examiner will then ask you some more questions about the situation.

Here is the situation:

You have been asked to make a presentation to staff about a new cleaning product the company is producing. Talk together for about two minutes about the things you think are important for the staff to know about the new product. Decide which three things are the most important.

Here are some ideas to help you:

- What it is for
- Who will use it
- Why it is a good product
- When it is available
- What it will cost
- What it is made from

Now go to page 97.

EXAM INFORMATION

In Part Three of the speaking test the interlocutor introduces a situation for you to discuss. There are pictures or short notes to help you. You are asked to discuss the situation together. You have about two minutes to do this and then the interlocutor will ask you more questions about it. The aim is to see how well you talk together, in particular, how you express opinions and agree and disagree with each other.

For this part of the test it is important to remember to:

- speak clearly to each other
- explain the reasons for your choices
- give your partner(s) a chance to speak.

A DETAILED STUDY

1   Read situation for Test 3 and complete the sentences with phrases **A–F**.

You have been asked to make a presentation to staff about a new cleaning product the company is producing. Talk together for about two minutes about the things you think are important for the staff to know about the new product. Decide which three things are the most important.

It's important for marketing staff to know:

1   what you can clean with it …

2   who will use it …

3   why it is a good product …

4   when it is available …

5   what it will cost …

6   what it is made from …

A   because customers will want to know if it is safe to use.

B   because customers will want to know if they can afford to buy it.

C   because it will affect where they advertize it.

D   because they will feel happier about marketing it.

E   because they need to decide when to start their marketing campaign.

F   because it will affect what information is in the instructions.

2   Decide which of the phrases below show you agree or disagree with your partner and which can help your partner to speak. Write **A** (agree), **D** (disagree) or **H** (help) next to each phrase.

1   What do you think?

2   You may be right but …

3   I think the same.

4   What's your opinion?

5   Absolutely.

6   I don't think so.

7   I don't agree.

8   Do you agree?

9   You're right.

Now look again at the situation in Part Three of the speaking test.

TEST FOUR

READING AND WRITING 1 hour 30 minutes

PART ONE

Questions 1–5

- *Look at questions **1–5**.*

- *In each question, which sentence is correct?*

- *For each question, mark one letter (**A, B** or **C**).*

Example:

0

| Susan's arriving at 8.45pm tomorrow. Can you collect her from the station? |

Susan arrives at

A   quarter to eight tomorrow morning.

B   quarter to nine tomorrow evening.

C   quarter to nine tomorrow morning.

The correct answer is **B**, so mark your answer sheet like this:

1

┌─────────────────────────────────┐

ALL CLERICAL STAFF

In case of a problem with
any office equipment, advise
your Supervisor, who will call
in the Technical Department
if necessary.

└─────────────────────────────────┘

Members of the clerical staff are expected to

A   deal with minor problems to their equipment.

B   ask their Supervisor to see to the problem.

C   get help from the Technical Department.

2

Product	Self-adhesive labels	Labels per sheet	21
Size	63.5mm x 38.1mm	Sheets per pack	100
Ref no	01684583	Labels per pack	2,100
Colour	yellow		

The pack contains

A   21 labels.

B   100 labels.

C   2,100 labels.

3

CADECO UK

Industrial Software Solutions

Alan Ball

Head of Technical Services

Cadeco House
Dawley Bank
Telford TF3 6HH

Tel: 01952 998000
Fax: 01952 998001

Head Office   CADECO USA   Balboa Cyn   San Diego CA 92102
Tel: 858 300 4000   Fax: 858 300 4011

Alan needs to discuss a technical problem with Head Office. Which number does he call?

A   01952 998000

B   858 300 4011

C   858 300 4000

4

Bill
Have you spoken to Annie yet? I meant to, but forgot! Sorry.
Sarah

A   Sarah wants Bill to phone Annie.

B   Sarah has forgotten to phone Bill.

C   Sarah wonders if Annie has phoned Bill yet.

5

Delivery
- orders over $75.00 free; otherwise charged at normal postal rates
- express delivery, $25.00 surcharge on all packages
- delivery within country only

You will have to pay delivery charges on

A   goods worth more than $75.00.

B   goods sent express.

C   goods sent overseas.

PART TWO

Questions 6–10

- *Look at these office documents.*

- *For questions **6–10**, decide which document (**A–H**) on the opposite page you would need to use.*

- *For each question, mark the correct letter (**A–H**).*

- *Do not use any letter more than once.*

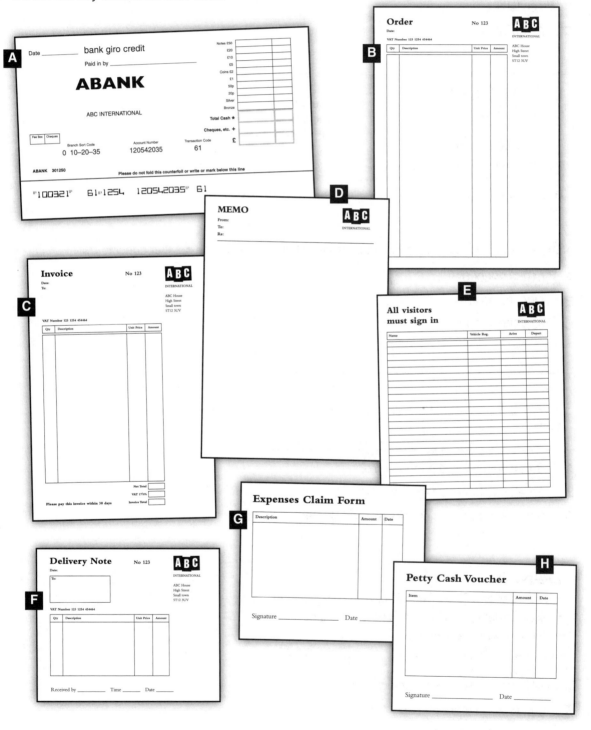

6   You need some money to buy coffee and milk for the office.

7   You need some stationery items, such as paper and envelopes.

8   Your company owes you money that you spent on travel and accommodation.

9   You sign this to show that you have received goods that have been sent to you.

10   This gives details of visitors to your company, e.g. name, date and time of arrival.

PART THREE

Questions 11–15

- *Look at the graphs below. They show the sales of electric and petrol-driven grass mowers by eight retailers lettered **A–H**, over a twelve-month period.*

- *Which graph does each sentence (**11–15**) on the opposite page describe?*

- *For each sentence, mark one letter (**A–H**).*

- *Do not use any letter more than once.*

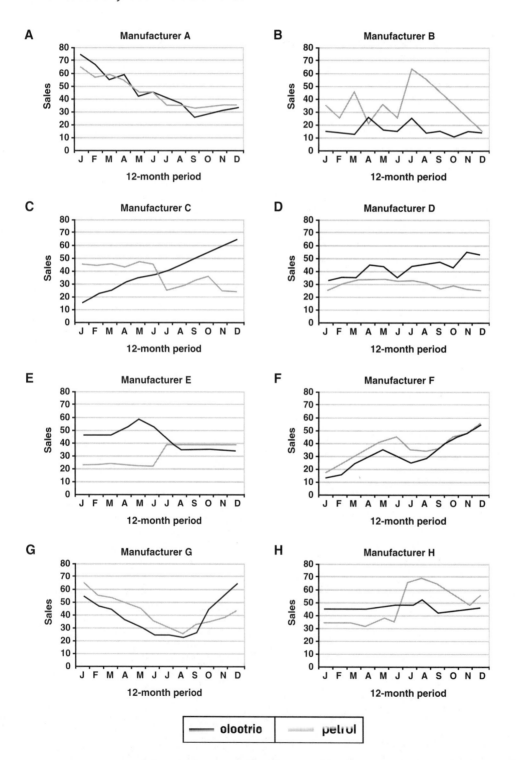

11   Sales of both types fell continuously until new models were introduced in August, after which sales, especially of electric mowers, picked up really well.

12   The number of electric mowers sold remained low all year, while petrol mower sales fell in the second half of the year from a peak in July.

13   After falling steadily for most of the year, sales of both electric and petrol mowers improved with the number of sales of manual mowers finally doing better than electric.

14   Electric mower sales improved steadily throughout the year, overtaking petrol mower sales in July.

15   Sales of both types were roughly the same, improving throughout the year apart from a slight dip in the period May–July.

PART FOUR

Questions 16–22

- *Read the following newspaper report about a contest for the best receptionist.*

- *Are the sentences **16–22** on the opposite page right or wrong? If there is not enough information to answer 'Right' or 'Wrong', choose 'Doesn't Say'.*

- *For each sentence **16–22**, mark one letter (**A**, **B** or **C**).*

Contest to find the Best Receptionist of the Year

5 The six contestants who reached the finals were invited to the National Press Office, where the final judging took place.

They took part in four tests: telephone
10 role plays; dealing with suspicious packages; a written test; and an interview. Telephone role plays included dealing with angry callers and with policemen asking for specific
15 information. In the written test, the finalists had to keep a record of a series of scheduled visitors and of several unexpected incidents. The hardest part for the contestants was keeping their
20 records tidy. Dealing with suspicious packages, for example, a parcel or letter which might contain something dangerous, was also difficult. Very few companies offer training in this and
25 only one of the contestants performed well on this task. For the last test, the judges interviewed each finalist in turn, asking them questions about their jobs.

30 Marks were awarded for each test and then added together to give a final score. Not surprisingly, the final scores were very close. Because the scores of the successful contestant, Ms Suzanne
35 Burdette, and the runner-up, Mr Ahmed Shawad, were only two points apart, the judges interviewed them both again before making a final decision.

16 The final judging of the *Best Receptionist of the Year* took place in London.

    A   Right   **B**   Wrong   **C**   Doesn't say

17 Part of the phone test was to measure how clearly the contestants spoke.

    A   Right   **B**   Wrong   **C**   Doesn't say

18 In the written test, the contestants dealt with both planned and unplanned events.

    A   Right   **B**   Wrong   **C**   Doesn't say

19 Some of the contestants had received training in handling suspicious packages.

    A   Right   **B**   Wrong   **C**   Doesn't say

20 The finalists were interviewed separately.

    A   Right   **B**   Wrong   **C**   Doesn't say

21 Because the final scores were close, all the contestants were re-interviewed.

    A   Right   **B**   Wrong   **C**   Doesn't say

22 The title *Best Receptionist of the Year* went to a woman.

    A   Right   **B**   Wrong   **C**   Doesn't say

PART FIVE
Questions 23–28

- *Read the reference below.*

- *For each question 23–28 on the opposite page, choose the correct answer.*

- *Mark one letter (A, B or C).*

Reference for Melinda Kleeger

Melinda Kleeger joined us in 1999 as Assistant Office Manager. During her time in that post, she dealt mainly with work conditions, and made many changes to improve the working environment, such as better office layout and lighting, and
5   better ventilation and air quality. We could not put all her ideas into practice, mainly because of cost, but staff conditions improved because of the changes which we did make. Our records show that time lost through illness and minor accidents went down after 1999, which must be due to the improvements that Melinda fought for.

10   In May 2002, the company created a new post: Health and Safety Officer. The post was advertised nationally. Ms Kleeger reached the short list of candidates to be interviewed, not because she was our employee, but because she was a strong candidate. She was easily the best-qualified in terms of experience, but she lacked qualifications specific to H&S. She got the job, but on the condition that she took a
15   training course leading to the Health and Safety Diploma. She passed easily, and took up her new post in September 2002.

Her new duties gave her responsibility for H&S not only in administration, where she had worked until now, but also in new areas such as production and distribution. She is a quick learner and was soon making recommendations in the
20   factory, including better safety clothing for operatives and better protective guards on dangerous machinery. An untidy workplace is a dangerous workplace, so she introduced new rules for keeping work areas clean and tidy. She changed the work rotas for operators of mobile equipment, making them take more frequent breaks to reduce accidents caused by tiredness.

25   Change is not always popular, but Melinda is very good with people. She has a wonderful ability to present her ideas in such a way that people come to believe that it was their idea in the first place! Once again, as a result of her work, loss of work time through accidents was reduced.

We are sorry to lose Melinda, but we understand that after six years with our
30   company she is ready to take on greater responsibilities. We are happy to support her application.

23   Why did the company not use some of Melinda's ideas?

     A   They were not very practical.

     B   The staff were against them.

     C   The company could not afford them.

24   One of the Melinda's improvements as Assistant Office Manager was to

     A   install air-conditioning.

     B   introduce more modern office machines.

     C   let staff personalize their work stations.

25   One result of Melinda's changes was that

     A   the staff worked much harder.

     B   the company could reduce the workforce.

     C   there were fewer staff absences.

26   Melinda got the job as Health and Safety Officer because

     A   she was already a member of the firm.

     B   she had a lot of experience in this area.

     C   she had a diploma in the subject.

27   One way Melinda tried to improve safety in the factory was by

     A   introducing safety clothing for factory workers.

     B   employing guards to check on dangerous equipment.

     C   making sure that work areas were kept clean.

28   In what way was Melinda 'good with people'?

     A   She could persuade people to accept in her ideas.

     B   She always listened carefully to what people had to say.

     C   People respected her because she knew her job very well.

PART SIX

Questions 29–40

- *Read the article below about a health problem (known as RSI) that keyboard users often have.*

- *Choose the correct word to fill each gap, from **A**, **B** or **C** on the opposite page.*

- *For each question **29–40**, mark one letter (**A**, **B** or **C**).*

RSI: Health Problems at the Keyboard

Do you use a keyboard in your job? If you **(29)** ...., you will at some time suffer 'RSI', that is, pain in **(30)** .... arms. What can you do **(31)** .... it? You can use an ice pack, or you could wear wrist supports **(32)** .... the ones that tennis players use.

Wrist supports **(33)** .... the wrist muscles warm, and prevent the injury from getting **(34)** .... You could also try **(35)** .... one of the new Maltron 'anti-RSI' keyboards.

People who use a Maltron keyboard say they no **(36)** .... get any pain.

Using your 'mouse' can also **(37)** .... problems. **(38)** .... you get a lot of pain in your 'mouse hand', try a Logitech mouse. That's the one with the ball on the top rather **(39)** .... underneath, so you just move your fingertips.

Finally, don't **(40)** .... too long at your keyboard: take a break every half hour!

29 **A** do   **B** make   **C** have

30 **A** your   **B** their   **C** her

31 **A** with   **B** about   **C** from

32 **A** as   **B** such   **C** like

33 **A** hold   **B** bring   **C** keep

34 **A** worse   **B** bad   **C** worst

35 **A** use   **B** using   **C** used

36 **A** more   **B** longer   **C** less

37 **A** cause   **B** get   **C** find

38 **A** So   **B** While   **C** If

39 **A** than   **B** then   **C** when

40 **A** make   **B** spend   **C** bring

PART SEVEN

Questions 41–45

- *Read the memo and the leaflet below.*

- *Complete the form on the opposite page.*

- *Write a word or phrase (in CAPITAL LETTERS) or a number on lines 41–45.*

Memo

From Caroline Booth, Administration

To   Peter Sparks, Purchasing

Re   Printing calculators

Now that each of our five departments has to keep careful financial records, please buy five printing calculators, plus one spare. Choose a model that has tax and euro functions (see attached). No need to open an account with these suppliers: pay COD, but insist that the goods are sent within three days of receipt of our order.

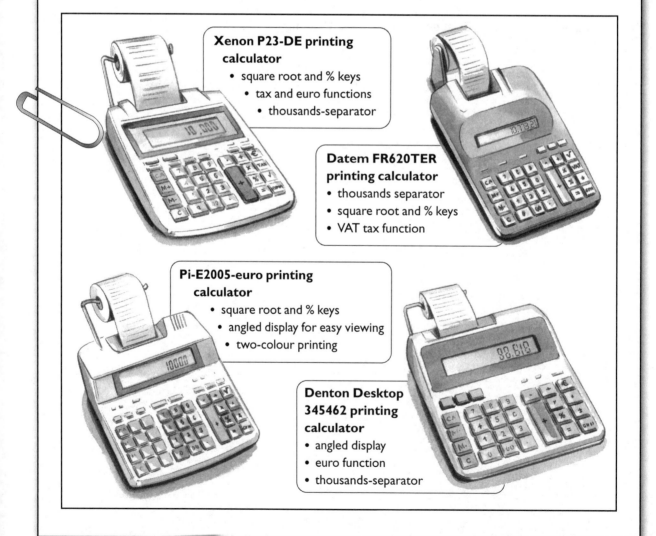

Xenon P23-DE printing calculator
- square root and % keys
- tax and euro functions
- thousands-separator

Datem FR620TER printing calculator
- thousands separator
- square root and % keys
- VAT tax function

Pi-E2005-euro printing calculator
- square root and % keys
- angled display for easy viewing
- two-colour printing

Denton Desktop 345462 printing calculator
- angled display
- euro function
- thousands-separator

ORDER FORM

Model make and number   **(41)** ....

Special feature(s) required   **(42)** ....

Quantity   **(43)** ....

Payment method   **(44)** ....

Delivery   **(45)** ....

Before you check your answers, go to page 112.

EXAM INFORMATION

The purpose of Part Seven of the reading test is to see if you can find information in a short text (or sometimes two texts) and then enter that information **accurately** in a form. The text(s) may be:

- office memos
- advertisements
- extracts from catalogues, directories, etc
- notices giving an instruction, a warning or other information.

The information may be:

- a single word, phrase or sentence such as a name, a specification
- a number, such as a telephone number, a date, a sum of money
- a mixture of numbers and letters, such as a catalogue number, an address.

The form where you have to write down the information may be:

- an order form
- a standard office form
- an invoice
- a file note
- a record of a phone call.

The form has five gaps, numbered **41–45,** and you must write your answers in capital letters.

A DETAILED STUDY

1   It is important to be careful in reading words and numbers from the text, and accurate in writing them. Look at the following items, compare them with the text on page 100, and see if there are any mistakes.

   1   Peter Sparkes is in Purchasing.

   2   Caroline Booth is in Administration

   3   The Xennon P23-DE printing calculator has square root and % keys.

   4   The P23-DE also has a thousands-seperator.

   5   The Datem FR820TEP has a VAT tax function.

   6   If you want an angled display, the Denton Desktop 345462 is the one for you.

2   The question below will help you understand the text better and make sure you choose the correct options for questions **41–45.**

   1   Why do the departments need printing calculators?

   2   Who will order the calculators?

   3   Which calculator has two-colour printing?

   4   What are the special features of the Denton Desktop calculator?

   5   Does the company have an account with the supplier?

   6   What do the letters COD stand for and what does the expression mean?

   7   What does the expression *within three days* mean?

   8   Complete this sentence: *The word 'receipt' comes from the verb 'to ...'*

Now check your answers to Part Seven of the reading test.

WRITING

PART ONE

Question 46

- *You cannot keep an appointment that you have made with your colleague Mizuki Goto in another branch of the firm.*

- *Write your colleague a **note**:*

    - *apologizing*

    - *explaining why you cannot keep the appointment*

    - *suggesting an alternative date and time for the meeting.*

- *Write **30–40** words.*

My dear Mizuki

....

....

....

....

....

....

....

....

....

Before you write the note, go to page 114.

A DETAILED STUDY

You cannot keep an appointment that you have made with your colleague Mizuki Goto in another branch of the firm. To help you understand the task, answer these questions.

1   What is the difference between:

    A   an *appointment* and a *date*?

    B   a *colleague* and a *friend*?

    C   a *branch* and a *department*?

    D   *Dear Mizuki* and *My dear Mizuki*?

2   Which of these expressions do you think would fit best in your note?

    A   **To apologize**

        I am sorry that I won't be able to …

        I regret that I won't be able to …

        There's no way I will be able to …

    B   **To explain**

        The reason is that I have to ...

        The thing is I have to ...

        It's because I have to ...

    C   **To make a suggestion**

        I suggest that we ...

        Why don't we ...

        Do you think we could ...

    D   **To finish off your note**

        Please let me know

        Love and kisses

        Yours faithfully

        I look forward to hearing from you.

Now write your own answer to question 46 in Part One of the writing test. Remember to check for grammar and spelling mistakes.

FOLLOW UP ACTIVITY

Look again at the answer you wrote for Question 46 and answer these questions.

1   Underline the words in your note to Mizuki that:

- apologize for having to change the meeting

- explain why you couldn't keep the original appointment

- suggest an alternative date and time.

2   Your note begins *My dear Mizuki*. How did you end the letter?

PART TWO
Question 47

- *Read this part of a letter offering to design a website for your company.*

As you can see from the attached brochure, we have designed websites for a wide range of industries from electronics to food processing. We invite you to visit some of the websites listed in the brochure to see for yourself the high standard of our work.

In addition to website design, we can provide help with registering domain names, finding a suitable ISP, etc.

We would be happy to discuss your requirements with you, without obligation on either side, and look forward to hearing from you.

Yours faithfully

A Costa

Adriana Costa
Marketing

email: acosta@webstart.com

- *Write an **email** to Adriana Costa:*

  - *thanking her for what she sent*

  - *expressing an interest in using her company's services*

  - *saying why your company wants a website*

  - *suggesting a meeting to discuss the matter.*

- *Write **60–80** words.*

- *Do not include postal addresses.*

LISTENING   40 minutes

PART ONE

Questions 1–8

Before you answer questions 1–8, go to page 119.

- *For questions **1–8** you will hear eight short recordings.*

- *For each question, mark **one** letter (**A**, **B** or **C**) for the most suitable picture or phrase.*

Example:

What did the sign say?

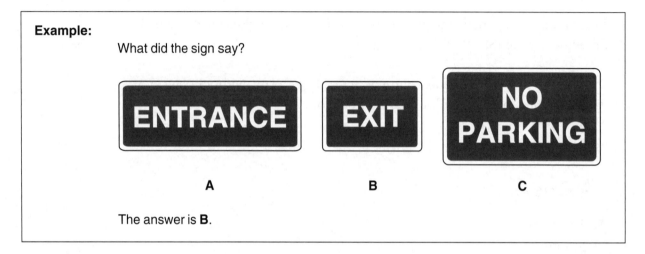

         A   **B**   **C**

The answer is **B**.

---

1   What time does the meeting begin?

     A   12 o'clock

     B   10 o'clock

     C   2 o'clock

2   Who has just left?

     A   the manager

     B   the chief executive

     C   the personal assistant

3   What has broken down?

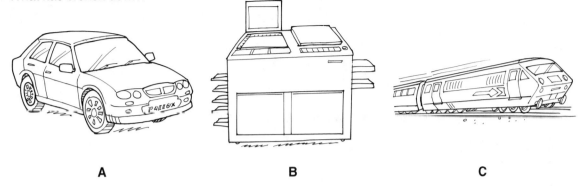

A   B   C

4   Where is Mr Wong?

   A   at his hotel

   B   in a restaurant

   C   in his office

5   Which is the correct graph?

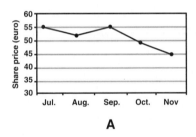

A

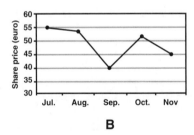

B

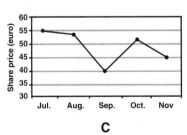

C

6   What has the company stopped producing?

   A   cars

   B   trucks

   C   motorbikes

7   What was the price of ACME's shares yesterday?

   A $2.37

   B $2.49

   C $2.50

8   Where is the directors' meeting?

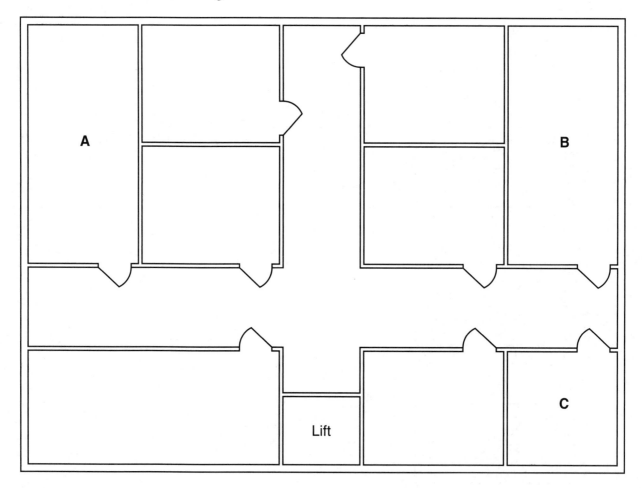

A DETAILED STUDY

In Part One of the listening test the questions have very short pieces of text to go with them, so you need to be well prepared. It is therefore very important to look at the questions carefully and decide what you are listening out for.

1   Read through the list below and decide for each question, **1–8**, what you are listening for.

- date
- time
- place
- person
- price
- object
- number
- activity
- trend
- sign
- message

1 _____

2 _____

3 _____

4 _____

5 _____

6 _____

7 _____

8 _____

2   Listen to the recording for Part One once only and decide for each question what the situation is about. You will need to use some descriptions from the list more than once.

- money
- giving directions
- asking permission
- products
- arrangements
- asking for information

1 _____

2 _____

3 _____

4 _____

5 _____

6 _____

7 _____

8 _____

Now you are ready to listen again to Part One of the listening test and answer questions 1–8.

PART TWO

Questions 9–15

- *Look at the notes below.*

- *Some information is missing.*

- *You will hear a woman asking about Freshlands Supermarkets.*

- *For each question **9–15**, fill in the missing information in the numbered space using a **time**, **numbers** or **letters**.*

FRESHFIELDS SUPERMARKETS

First store opened in: **(9)** ....

Location of first store: **(10)** ....

Number of stores in the North: **(11)** ....

Number of stores opening in 2005:   **(12)** ....

Average number of staff at each store: **(13)** ....

Total number of staff: **(14)** ....

Percentage of food retail market: **(15)** ....

PART THREE
Questions 16–22

- *Look at the notes below.*

- *Some information is missing.*

- *You will hear the managing director of a hotel chain talking to her staff on a training day.*

- *For each question **16–22**, fill in the missing Information in the numbered space using **one** or **two** words.*

MARLBOROUGH HOTELS

Staff Training Day (18ᵗʰ October 2004)
Introductory Speech

Points to mention:

- Express thanks to all staff for successful summer season.

- Refurbishment of lounges and private **(16)** .... completed.

- Good summer for hotels and outside catering: lots of **(17)** .... this year.

- Our **(18)** .... (thank Jamie personally) has been extremely successful in attracting new customers: due to exciting, new dishes.

- **(19)** .... increase in non residents in restaurants.

- New appointment: Jontje Lister as **(20)** .... who has had many years of hospitality experience in **(21)** ....

- Exciting initiative to welcome **(22)** .... and their owners.

PART FOUR
Questions 23–30

- *You will hear a presentation given by a management consultant.*

- *For each question 23–30, mark one letter (A, B or C) for the correct answer.*

23   According to the consultant, what did chief executives have to do in the past when making a speech?

   A   get a good speech-writer

   B   smile at the audience a lot

   C   not talk for too long

24   If you are interviewed by a TV reporter, remember to

   A   refer to your company brochure.

   B   give lots of information about the company.

   C   sound as natural as possible.

25   Be aware that a TV interview is really

   A   a presentation.

   B   a conversation.

   C   a report.

26   When you are asked about a decision the company has made, always

   A   explain the reasons behind it.

   B   keep to the most important points.

   C   know how much time you have left.

27   It's a good idea if you can accept that being interviewed by a TV reporter is

    A   a risk that you should avoid if possible.

    B   an opportunity to tell people about your company.

    C   a necessity if you are to do your job properly.

28   Early on in the interview it's important to

    A   say something positive about your company.

    B   greet the interviewer politely.

    C   get your message across to the viewers.

29   You must learn how to deal with questions that are

    A   difficult.

    B   interesting.

    C   hidden.

30   You can only really relax

    A   when the camera light is off.

    B   when the interview has ended.

    C   when you are driving home.

SPEAKING 12 minutes

PART ONE (ABOUT 2 MINUTES)

In this part of the test the examiner (interlocutor) will ask each of you some questions about where you work or study, where you live or what you do in your free time. Here are some sample questions:

- What do you like/dislike about your job/studies?
- Would you like to change anything about your job/studies?
- Why is that?
- Where do you live?
- What do you like about living in a town/village/the countryside?
- Would you prefer to live somewhere else?
- Can you tell me more about that?

PART TWO (ABOUT FIVE MINUTES)

In this part of the test you are asked to give a 'mini presentation'. You have a choice of topic such as those below and you have one minute to prepare what you are going to say. After you have spoken, the examiner will ask your partner to say something about what you have said. After you have listened to your partner's presentation, the examiner will ask you to say something about what your partner has said.

Prompt Card (a) *(Given to Candidate A, and a copy to Candidate B)*

A: WHAT IS IMPORTANT WHEN ...?

Booking a hotel room

- Length of stay

- Type of room

- Cost

Prompt Card (b) *(Given to Candidate B, and a copy to Candidate A)*

B: WHAT IS IMPORTANT WHEN ...?

Responding to a complaint

- An apology

- An explanation

- Compensation

PART THREE (ABOUT 5 MINUTES)

The examiner will describe a situation to you and give you a few prompts to help you. You are asked to discuss the situation with your partner. You have 30 seconds to look at the prompt card and two minutes to discuss the situation. The examiner will then ask you some more questions about the situation.

Here is the situation:

A European company which imports coffee is sending someone on a business trip to Africa. Discuss together what the person needs to take and decide which three things are the most important.

Here are some ideas to help you:

Now go to page 126.

EXAM INFORMATION

In Part Three of the speaking test, when you have discussed the situation with your partner, the interlocutor will ask each of you some general questions about the topic. The interlocutor will make sure that you both have a chance to answer. This part of the test is to give you the opportunity to show you can give a fully developed answer on a business topic.

A DETAILED STUDY

Read the situation for Test 4 again and complete the answers below. You can use phrases from the box to help you.

A European company that imports coffee is sending someone on a business trip to Africa. Discuss together what the person needs to take and decide which three things are the most important.

> very tiring　　visiting new places is exciting　　helps you understand other ways of doing business
>
> waste of time　　deal with problems more easily　　waste of money
>
> good to do business face to face　　saves time　　saves money　　never been there
>
> have a different way of doing things　　understand each other better
>
> dont like travelling very much anyway

1　Would you like to go on a business trip abroad? (Why/Why not?)

    A　Yes, I would. I think it would make my job more interesting.

    B　No, I wouldn't. I …

2　How useful do you think business trips are? (Why/Why not?)

    A　I think they could be very useful because …

    B　Not very useful …

3　Do you think companies think that business trips are essential?

    A　Yes, they do because …

    B　Not all of them. Some companies think that business trips …

4　What countries would you like to visit on business? (Why?)

    I'd like to …

5　What do you think is important about visiting your customers abroad?

    If you actually meet your customers …

KEY AND EXPLANATION

TEST ONE

p.6–7   READING   Part 1

1   **A:** The key word is *except*. All personal calls must be made on the payphone, but if the call is about an emergency, you can use an office phone.
   B: The notice does not say where you must make an emergency call.
   C: The payphone is in Reception.

2   **C:** This is the copier that does most pages per minute and takes the least time to produce the first copy.

3   **C:** Dalmian must deliver the goods *within seven days*. If not, they will lose the order as their customers will go to *another supplier*.
   A: Dalmian must deliver the goods, not get them from another company.
   B: The email refers to a past phone conversation. It does not ask for delivery to be confirmed by phone.

4   **A:** The working days are: Tuesday 11, Wednesday 12, Friday 14, Monday 17 and Tuesday 18. All the other days are either free or for travel.

5   **B:** *Reschedule* is another way of saying *rearrange*, that is, have the meeting at a different time.
   A: It is Arturo who wants Debbie to phone Mr Partridge to reschedule the meeting.
   C: Mr Partridge has already spoken to Arturo to explain that he is *held up in heavy traffic*.

FURTHER PRACTICE AND GUIDANCE (p.8)

A Detailed Study

1   1   notice
    2   information
    3   email
    4   diary
    5   phone message

2   **Question 1**
    1   T   and if it is personal, you may use an office phone.
    2   T
   Question 2
    3   F   it is the slowest (10.5 seconds to make the first copy)
    4   T   see second column, *Pages per minute*
   Question 3
    5   F   it is about receiving goods from Dalmain
    6   F   only if they are not delivered on time

Question 4
   7   T
   8   F   she is going from Amanha to Rio by car, but it doesn't say how she will get back to Rio
Question 5
   9   F   Arturo is sending a note to Debbie
   10   T   he is held up in heavy traffic and is on his mobile phone

p.9–10   READING   Part 2

6   **B:** A secure cash box, i.e., one that you can lock, is the place to put money.

7   **F:** To avoid back pain, you need to support your back with a specially designed cushion.

8   **C:** A way to get rid of the dust is to use an extractor fan.

9   **A:** Michel can use the fluid to clean up the mess he has made.

10   **H:** A storage wallet has plastic pockets into which you put CDs.

p.11   READING   Part 3

11   **D:** Charts with the three poorest years are D, F and H, but only chart D fits the information about sales *picking up briefly in the third quarter*.

12   **A:** The phrase *a very uneven year* could apply to all the charts except F, but chart A is the only one which had *good results in the middle two quarters*.

13   **G:** Charts for A, D, E, G and H all show *a poor start*. Sales were *at record levels* for charts E and G, but it is chart G that shows *the fourth quarter beating all records*.

14   **C:** Charts C, E and G could all show *a very good year*, but only chart C shows *a disastrous fall in business between April and June*.

15   **E:** Both charts D and E had a start to the year which could *be the worst start ... in living memory*, and both had higher sales in the third quarter, but only chart E shows *an amazing peak in the third quarter*.

p.12–13   READING   Part 4

16   **A:** The key phrase is *There's no minimum size of order* (line 14), which means that they will accept even very small orders.

17 B: The program is free. It is the registration fee that costs €25. (line 5)

18 A: The key words are *5% handling charge for payment by cheque.* (lines 15–16)

19 C: There is no mention of **how** the delivery charge can be paid.

20 C: The key phrase is *Mac users, email ... for instructions* (lines 22–24). We cannot be sure what that means.

21 A: The key phrase is *all leading domestic and foreign makes* (line 7). The word *leading* here means the most common or popular makes of vehicle.

22 A: The key words are *Online Support.* (line 17)

FURTHER PRACTICE AND GUIDANCE (p.14–15)

A Detailed Study

1 **1** They supply spare parts for vehicles.
   2 You can download it from their website.
   3 They cover all leading domestic and foreign makes.
   4 They will usually deliver within 48 hours of receiving the order.
   5 They offer discounts on all leading domestic makes, and on many foreign makes.
   6 They will accept orders of any value.
   7 The company has an online support service on its website and a helpline.
   8 You must have Windows 98 or later and 5Mb of hard disk space.

2 **9** Wrong: the website address is *co.uk.*
   10 Doesn't say: they say *you will be lucky to find a cheaper supplier,* but we don't know if they will always be cheaper.
   11 Wrong: you can also pay by credit card.
   12 Doesn't say: all it says is that Mac users must phone for instructions. We don't know what that means.
   13 Doesn't say: the company probably deals with overseas customers too, but the text doesn't say so.
   14 Wrong: the company will *refund* [the registration fee] *with your first order,* which must mean that you can register before you place an order.
   15 Wrong: the text says you need Windows 98 or later, but we don't know if it will work **better** with later versions than Windows 98.

p.16–17 READING Part 5

23 C: Interprise matches companies because it *helps businesses to find partners ...* (lines 8–9)
   A: The text says *it isn't the word 'enterprise' spelled wrongly!* (lines 2–3).
   B: The text says it is **like** a dating agency. (lines 5–6)

24 B: The text says that the host companies *say what kind of **partner** they are looking for.* (lines 33–34)
   A: Interprise events are **not** trade fairs (line 50), so the purpose of these events is not buying and selling.
   C: People travel to get to the events but this is not the **purpose** of the event.

25 C: The catalogue is produced in order to publicize *the **coming** event.* (lines 25–26)
   A + B: Catalogues may also be distributed during and after the event but this is not mentioned in the text.

26 B: The text says that each EU partner (usually a Chamber of Commerce) is *expected to bring at least fifteen companies.* (lines 44–45)
   A: This is not mentioned in the text. The Chambers of Commerce are themselves 'visitors' to the event.
   C: Interprise organizes the event.

27 B: The text says *everything is carefully arranged in advance.* (lines 55–56)
   A: This is true of both kinds of event.
   C: It is true that the EU pays for part of the running costs, but it may be that the EU helps to fund trade fairs too.

28 A: The comments at the end of the text (lines 62–66) refer to making contacts.
   B: There is no reference to promoting the business in the text.
   C: One company says it has found some firms that are interested in becoming distributors, not that they distributed their product.

p.18–19 READING Part 6

29 B: *X days a week* is a set phrase. Here it means five and a half days out of a week of seven days.

30 B: *Need* is followed by *to*: ***need to** be able. Can be able* does not make sense in this context.

31 C: In the positive form, the pattern is *as ... as.* It is only in the negative that you can say *as ... as* **or** *so ... as,* for example: *I am not **as/so** clever as Jane.* And *well as* does not make sense.

32 A: The plural *them* is needed to agree with *are university graduates.*

33 C: This is a passive form: *be* + past participle. The word *seen* here means *considered, thought of.*

34 A: The difference of these three words can be seen in a phrase like *run until you drop*. *Until* means *up to the moment in the future when something happens*. It would make no sense to say *run when you drop* or *run while you drop*.

35 C: You *earn* money and you *win* a game, competition or prize. *To gain* means *to get* but usually in the sense of *to get more of something,* for example: *to gain experience*.

36 C: You use *any* after a negative or a simple question form: *they don't get **any** more; will they get **any** more?* You use *some* in positive sentences: *I want **some** more information,* or in questions which are really more like suggestions or offers: *Would you like **some** more cake?*

37 A: *Work for your money* means *work in order to get your money*. This is a set phrase. *work with* means *work together with*: *I like the people I **work with**. To work to* means *following*: *We are all **working to** the same plan.*

38 B: *Up to* means *as far as that point but not any farther,* i.e., they do not cover you for more than 50% of the costs.

39 A: *Can* and *could* are followed by the base form of the verb without *to*, for example: *You can **do** it. I couldn't **help** it.*

40 A: You use *even* to say that something may surprise you, for example: *I don't like dogs: I won't **even** go into a house where a dog has been.*

p.20–21   READING   Part 7

41 IRMGARD RUCHTI
She is the subject of Peter Madsen's email to Willi Epp.

42 SECURITY
She is the deputy head of security.

43 24th–27th JUNE [INCLUSIVE]
The word *inclusive* means that the time includes the starting date (24th) and the ending date (27th), i.e., four days.

44 [JOB] INTERVIEW
The words *interview* and *post* in Willi's note to Rolf tell us that she has a job interview.

45 09922 232232
This is the number given in Peter's email to Willi. The number 4545 is Peter's extension.

p.22   WRITING   Part 1

46 Model answer

MEMO

To: Tansu Ordek
From: ....
Date: 24 October
Re: <u>Office Equipment Exhibition</u>

The annual Splendida Exhibition is in Bilbao this year, from 17–20 November. As we intend to replace our older machines, I request your permission to attend in order to see the latest products.

(40 words)

The memo covers all the points:
- you have explained why you think the exhibition is important: *As we intend to replace our older machines, … in order to see the latest products.*
- you have requested permission to attend: *I request your permission to attend*
- you have said where and when the exhibition takes place: *in Bilbao, from 17–20 November.*

FURTHER PRACTICE AND GUIDANCE (p.23–24)

Exam Information

1 G	2 D	3 A	4 E	5 B	6 H
7 I	8 C	9 F	10 J		

A Detailed Study

1. Once a year. The key word is *annual*.
2. No. The key words are *This year*.
3. Five days. The key word is *inclusive*.
4. He wants to see what is new because his firm has to equip some new restaurants.
5. He doesn't directly ask permission. The phrase *I should attend to learn about the latest products* suggests that he is asking if he can go.
6. He can stay with his family instead of staying in a hotel.

p.25 WRITING Part 2

47 Model answer

To:	Ali Bardak
From:	
Re:	In house training services
Date:	
Pages:	1

Thank you for your fax inquiring about our training services. We would be very interested in helping you. We design courses for each client's specific needs, so it would be useful to know exactly which clerical skills you require. Could you also let us know how many of your staff need training? I suggest we have a meeting at your office as soon as convenient. I will phone you to fix date and time.

(74 words)

The fax covers all the points:
- you have thanked him: *Thank you for your fax inquiring ... services.*
- you have asked which clerical skills he is referring to: *it would be useful to know exactly which clerical skills you require.*
- you have asked for more information about numbers of staff: *Could you also let us know how many of your staff need training?*
- you have suggested a meeting: *I suggest we have a meeting at your office as soon as possible. I will phone you to fix date and time.*

p.26–27 LISTENING Part 1

1 **A:** *I've got to meet the directors at half-past six.*
B: She won't leave the office before half-past seven (after her appointment).
C: The film starts at eight, not the meeting.

2 **B:** *... but Head Office is moving to Belfast.* and *... they've decided to make Belfast the administrative centre.*
A: She is not moving to Belfast, she is staying in Dublin.
C: The company is opening a new store in Cork, not a new head office.

3 **C:** *You must go to gate seventeen immediately.*
A: He is already at the information desk because he heard an announcement.
B: He tells the woman that he has checked in, so he does not need to do this.

4 **A:** *I think he's gone for lunch.* and *I'm going over to the canteen now.*
B: There is a problem with car doors, but this is on the production line, not in the car park.
C: There is a call from the production line for Mr Fleming, so he must be somewhere else.

5 **C:** *Since April we've seen output increase from 30 to 60 thousand tonnes.*

6 **B:** *But, for the moment, the exchange rate is up from point nine three at the end of trading yesterday to point nine seven today.*
A: One euro may soon be worth one dollar, but it isn't yet.
C: A dollar was €0.93 yesterday, not today.

7 **B:** *Do you mean the flat screen monitor?*
A: The man made a mistake. He was looking at the wrong print-out when he said it was a computer.
C: The woman works for a printing service, but she did not leave a printer to be repaired.

8 **C:** *That'll be Customer Services.*
A: She asks if Mr Firth is the manager. She does not ask to speak to the manager.
B: The person who answers the phone is the operator, but that is not who she needs to speak to.

FURTHER PRACTICE AND GUIDANCE (p.28–29)

Part One: questions using graphs and charts

1	A iii	B i	C ii
2	A iii	B i	C ii
3	A iii	B i	C ii
4	A ii	B iii	C i

A Detailed Study

2   1   a time
     2   a place
     3   an action
     4   a place
     5   a trend
     6   a number
     7   an object
     8   a person

3   1   True
     2   False. She is not going to leave the office before half-past seven.
     3   False. It is the head office which is moving to Belfast.
     4   True
     5   True
     6   True
     7   False. It is the man who knows where Mr Fleming is.
     8   False. Steel production was low last year.
     9   True
     10   False. It may be worth a dollar at a later stage but not at the moment.
     11   False. They have fixed a lap-top but it does not belong to the woman.
     12   False. They do not offer to deliver but the woman says she will collect it.
     13   False. She has received a damaged parcel.
     14   True

p.30   LISTENING   Part 2

9   6: *Six then, fine.* (line 6)
Not 7. John asks if there are seven and is told: *One's dropped out.*

10   9.15: *When are they arriving? Nine-fifteen in reception.* (lines 6–7)
Not 9. John has to be waiting in reception before the interviewees arrive: *so be there by nine at the latest.*

11   10.00: *Interviews begin at ten.* (line 10)
Not 12. That is when Irina expects the interviews to finish: *so I should be through by twelve.*

12   20 minutes: *I expect to spend about twenty minutes with each of them …* (lines 11–12)

13   CONTI

14   1–2.30: *Then there's lunch. That'll be in the canteen between one and two-thirty.* (lines 24–25)
Not 12.30. Irina asks John to remind the chef they are coming: *Give the chef a ring at twelve-thirty …*

15   £300: *Three hundred pounds should cover it …* (line 37)
Not £100. That was the cost of the rail ticket for just one of the interviewees: *I know one person had to pay over a hundred pounds for a rail ticket.*

p.31   LISTENING   Part 3

16   1994: *… I started Agriproducts in 1994, after nearly twenty years working on the land.* (lines 6–7)

17   a farmer: *Being a farmer is a hard life but I loved it.* (lines 2–3)

18   meat: *I didn't know much about dairy products, so in the first five years we concentrated on finding markets for meat and animal feeds.* (lines 15–18)

19   was cheap: *We had plenty of space – land was still cheap.* (lines 20–21)

20   airports, railways: *The only major disadvantage was we were not very near to airports or railways.* (lines 22–24)

21   Spain: *In fact, the first country we exported to was Spain.* (lines 28–29)

22   England / home market, etc.: *Still, we're going to concentrate on the home market first and test the water.* (lines 40–42)

p.32–33   LISTENING   Part 4

23   **C:** The interviewer says *a very good manager. Someone who was able to do ten things at once and still appear cheerful and calm.* (lines 10–12)
A: Sharon is *cheerful and calm* but this is not enough to make her a good manager.
B: The interviewer says *Sharon was making a good job of my nails* but we do not know if she is a good beautician and anyway this is not the same as being a manager.

24   **B:** Sharon says *I like to know how people are getting on together. I watch everybody all the time.* (lines 19–21)
A: Sharon doesn't say she is a good manager because she gets on well with people.
C: Although Sharon keeps an eye on her staff, she doesn't say she has to tell them what to do.

25   **C:** Sharon says *the directors asked me to take over.* (lines 31–32)
A: She was doing a secretarial course, not a management course.
B: Her manager was off sick and did not recommend her.

26   **A:** Sharon says *the salon is in my name.* (line 37)
B: Her husband put some money into the business and does the accounts, but the business is not his.
C: Most of the money that went into the salon was left to Sharon by her father.

27   **C:** Sharon says *We opened properly in April …* (lines 44–45)
A: They should have opened in January but there was a fire.
B: They bought the premises in February.

28   **C:** Sharon says *…so there's five of us now.* (line 48)
A: She says that they will need two more staff by Christmas.
B: She says that she's taken on three assistants.

29   **A:** Sharon says *They need to know you will be kind and say the right thing.* (lines 62–63)
B: She says that they need to feel OK about spending time and money on themselves.
C: She does spend a lot of time with them but that is because of the treatment, not because she knows them well.

30   **A:** Sharon's job is like a doctor's because she helps to make her customers feel better. She says *I can make them feel better because they look better.* (lines 68–69)
B: She listens to their problems but she doesn't try to solve them.
C: She spends a lot of time on her clients but not just listening to them.

SPEAKING

FURTHER PRACTICE AND GUIDANCE (p.35–36)

A Detailed Study

1 **1** A answers the question fully. B does not give any information about what you **like**.

  2 B answers the question fully and gives a reason for wanting to live somewhere else. A does not give much information and where the sister lives is irrelevant.

  3 B is the most complete answer as it develops the answer by adding a relevant comment. A only gives one example. A is not well expressed.

  4 A answers the question fully and is well expressed. B does not answer the question: *If you had more time*.

2 **1** C   **2** F   **3** D   **4** A   **5** B

TEST TWO

p.38–39   READING   Part 1

1   **C:** The key phrase is *Confirm … with your Department Supervisor*. This means the same as *agreed by your superior*.
A: The holiday dates have to be confirmed by the supervisor **before** they can be added to the holiday list.
B: The notice only refers to the supervisor in the department.

2   **A:** The key phrase is *long or short lets* which means that the properties are for rent. A *flat* is the same as an *apartment*.
B: This agency does not sell houses, it rents them.
C: Hotels are not mentioned in the advertisement.

3   **A:** The only way to get a refund is to show your receipt.
B: The notice does not say you have to bring the packet of biscuits.
C: The notice refers to health reasons but it does not say that you have to be sick in order to get a refund.

4   **C:** Ottawa. The flight arrives at 17.45 and departs the next day at 14.00. Also, the note refers to a *stopover in Ottawa*.

5   **B:** You post your reply in the envelope they have sent you, which already has a stamp and the return address on it.
A: They are requesting a reply, not an envelope.
C: They are requesting a reply, which is why they have enclosed the envelope.

p.40–41   READING   Part 2

6   **G:** The key words are *all the computers are down*, that is, they are not working. You need technical support, the department responsible for repairing and servicing office equipment.

7   **D:** The key phrase is *you want it edited and printed*, that is, you want someone to do those things for you. The typing pool does those things.

8   **F:** The key phrase is *a one-day meeting*. For this meeting you will need the conference room.

9   **H:** The key phrase is *enough coffee, tea, sugar, etc.* These things are kept in the kitchen.

10   **B:** The key words phrase is *CV's of three members of staff*. Such documents will be kept by the personnel department.

FURTHER PRACTICE AND GUIDANCE (p.42)

A Detailed Study

1   1 D   2 A   3 G   4 B   5 E   6 C

2   1   False. *They are down* means *they are not working*.
    2   True
    3   True
    4   False. The word *refreshments* refers to food and drink other than a main meal.
    5   True

p.43–44   READING   Part 3

11   **D:** The key phrase is *a record number of serious injuries*; the chart for injuries shows that 1997 has the highest number of serious injuries.

12   **H:** The key phrase is *Time lost was up on previous years*. 2001 has the highest amount of time lost and also the greatest amount of time for medical treatment.

13   **C:** The phrase *very few serious injuries* could apply to 1995 or 1996; but the phrase *medical treatment was up 300% on the previous year* can only apply to 1996.

14   **E:** The phrase *serious injuries … well down on the previous year* could apply to 1995, 1996, 1998 or 2000; but the phrase *need for medical treatment doubled* only applies to 1998.

15   **B:** The phrase *time lost … half that of the previous year* could apply to 1995 or 1999; but the phrase *as was the number of serious injuries* can only apply to 1995.

FURTHER PRACTICE AND GUIDANCE (p.45)

A Detailed Study

1   1   a disastrous fall in business   W
    2   a peak in July   B
    3   a slight dip   W
    4   a slight increase   B
    5   began to fall off   W
    6   continued to grow steadily   B
    7   did equally well   S
    8   doubled   B
    9   falling steadily   W
    10   fell continuously   W
    11   gradually picked up   B
    12   remained steady   S
    13   fell in the second half   W
    14   roughly the same   S
    15   picked up well   B
    16   reached an amazing peak   B

17 sales were at record levels	B	
18 slightly ahead	B	
19 starting and finishing badly	S	
20 tailed off in the last quarter	W	
21 remained low all year	S	
22 down on the previous year	W	

2 **1** D (1997)   **2** C (1996)   **3** G (2000)
   4 H (2001)   **5** A (1994)

p.46–47   READING   Part 4

16 B: W Ibsley was not ill but on maternity leave. (line 7)

17 B: He says that employees should learn **either** Portuguese **or** Spanish, not both. (line 10)

18 C: The text only says that training managers should find out if any employees already knew a foreign language. (lines 14–15)

19 C: The text says **what** the working group will do (lines 19–20), but not **how** it will do its work.

20 A: The members of the working group (line 19), Allen, Douglas and Fairchild, were all present. (line 5)

21 C: There is no information about where the language courses will be.

22 A: One of the decisions was *each company … should be responsible for finding suitable materials and local providers of language training.* (lines 17–18)

p.48–49   READING   Part 5

23 C: She was *the first woman to have a seat on the New York Stock Exchange.* (lines 2–4)
A: She owned her own company but the text does not say that she was the first woman to do so.
B: She became a Superintendent of Banking, she did not run a bank.

24 B: She believes *Women executives can be a strong competitive force against other countries that still only employ males in executive positions.* (lines 11–14)
A: She believes women can offer *different viewpoints and experiences*, not that they are better than men.
C: She believes in taking risks but the text does not say that women in general are risk-takers.

25 A: She says *the real risk lies in continuing to do things the way they've always been done.* (lines 20–22)
B: The text says *In these fast-changing times we need different viewpoints and experiences* but it does not say that the worst risk is to change things too quickly.
C: The text makes no reference to employing more men.

26 A: The text refers to men she asked to sponsor her application (lines 27–29) and says *she needed a letter from a bank saying they would lend her …* (lines 31–33)
B: The text makes no reference to an application form, and in any case, if there were one, she would send it to the Stock Exchange, not to her bank.
C: To enter the Stock Exchange means to get a seat on the Stock Exchange; she rang the bell thirty years later. (lines 39–41)

27 C: The text says *Interest rates climbed steeply…* (lines 45–46)
A: The text refers to a bank president having to cut his salary in half but there is nothing in the text about wages in general being too high.
B: There were bank failures everywhere but this is not the same as banks not wanting to lend money.

28 A: The text says *three employees had left taking her customer lists with them* (lines 59–60). This means that they 'stole' the firm's customers.
B: The text says she rejected offers to buy her company but this was not what had gone wrong with her firm.
C: It is true that she still had to finish the job she had started but this is not why her company got into difficulties.

p.50–51   READING   Part 6

29 C: The pattern is *so* + adjective + *that* followed by the result, for example: *I am* **so tired that** *I cannot keep my eyes open. Very* + adjective makes a complete statement: *I am* **very tired**. The pattern with *too* is seen in *I am* **too tired** *to sleep*. This means the same as *I am so tired that I cannot sleep.*

30 A: You use *any* after the negative *nobody*.

31 A: You *suggest* something *to* someone. You *make a suggestion to* someone *about* something

32 B: *One* stands for *a* + noun, i.e., he doesn't want a mission statement. *It* would only be right if I had offered him a statement, not just the idea of having a statement: *I have written this for you. – Thank you, but I don't want* **it**. *Them* is the plural of *it* in this case and would also be wrong unless I had written **more** than one statement and offered them to him.

33 B: To *do nothing for* is a fixed expression. *It* **does nothing for** *me* means *I get no benefit of advantage from it.*

34 B: The *mission statement* is followed by third person singular, i.e., verb + -s.

35 A: Think of the statement *The company is trying to do something*. To ask a question about it, you would say **What** *is the company trying to do? What* replaces *something*. In indirect speech it is **Say what** *the company is trying to do.*

36 C: This is a passive form: *be* + past participle. The past participle of *write* is *written*, for example: *I have **written** several poems. Wrote* is the simple past: *I **wrote** this one for you yesterday.*

37 C: *Tesco, a … chain, describes … .* The verb is singular, so we need the possessive *its*, not *theirs*. Note that organizations are often thought of as plural, so you might find *The council has changed its plans* or *The council have changed their plans*. Both are correct, but do not 'mix' them. Avoid sentences like ~~The company is thinking of changing their mission statement.~~

38 A: Only *is* makes sense here. *It **is** a wonderful example of a mission statement.* You can say *it provides an example* but not *it ~~does~~ an example. It* refers to the mission statement, so we cannot say that the mission statement *has* a good example.

39 C: The clause **because** *the company is now the biggest … explains why we know that Tesco's mission statement has worked.

40 A: After a superlative (*-est* or *most …*), you use the preposition *in* before a place, for example: *the best **in** the world.*

p.52–53   READING   Part 7

41 PETTIVALE GARDEN SUPPLIES
Lakmi spoke to Michael Byers, who works for this company.

42 RT2124
This is the missing invoice. RT2123 was the previous invoice, the one that was issued twice.

43 MICHAEL BYERS
Lakmi says *make sure it goes to direct him, OK?*.

44 REPAIRS TO (VGS DELIVERY) VAN
This information is on the JOB form.

45 £494
Made up of the cost of parts, £144, plus the cost of labour, £350.

p.54   WRITING   Part 1

46 Model answer

> **Memo**
> **To**   John Oates
> **From**
> **RE**   Request for company car
>
> I have to visit clients in several cities but my own car has broken down so I need a company car. Can I have a big car, preferably automatic, for ten days, from 12-21 May?

(36 words)

The note covers all the points:
- you have explained your problem: *I have to visit clients in several cities but my own car has broken down.*
- you have requested a car: *so I need a company car.*
- you have said the kind of car and when you will need it: *a big car, preferably automatic, for ten days, from 12-21 May.*

p.55   WRITING   Part 2

47 Model answer

> Dear Ms Poilue
> Re: Your order #19445
> Thank you for your letter of 15 June, telling us that you received the wrong goods. We wish to apologize for this mistake on our part. As you said in your letter, two orders were mixed up, and you received goods which were intended for another company.
> The goods you ordered will be sent to you today by express post.
> There is no need to return the red wallets. Please accept them with our compliments.

(79 words)

The letter covers all the points:
- you have thanked her: *Thank you for your letter of*
- you have apologized: *We wish to apologize*
- you have explained what happened: *two orders were mixed up, and you received goods which were intended for another company.*
- you have said what you are going to do: *The goods will be sent to you today by express post.*
- The last two sentences inviting them to keep the red wallets without charge is another way of showing that you are sorry (and making up) for what has happened.

FURTHER PRACTICE AND GUIDANCE (p.56)

Exam Information

1 D   2 H   3 B   4 J   5 G   6 E   7 B
8 I   9 F   10 C

A Detailed Study

1   There should be an introductory sentence, such as *Thank you for your letter of [date].* There should be some kind of apology, such as *We are sorry for the inconvenience we have caused.*

2   The letter contains the following mistakes:

can ~~confirmed~~	can confirm
someone ~~else~~ order	someone else's order
will be ~~send~~	will be sent
~~acept~~	accept
We should like you to ~~keeping~~	We should like you to keep
that ~~we do~~	that we will do
~~aviod~~	avoid

p.57–59   LISTENING   Part 1

1   **C:** *I only ordered it on Friday*
A: The stationery usually arrives on a Monday (if it has been ordered in time).
B: They usually place the order on Thursday but this time they didn't.

2   **A:** *I was working for a government department.*
B: Chris is working for J P Engineering at the moment. We are told he joined the company last month.
C: The woman thought that Chris used to work for Ashlings but Chris corrects her. He was offered a job with Ashlings but he didn't take it.

3   **B:** *So I've decided to open our first food hall.*
A: The range of children's wear is new but it has already been introduced.
C: The perfume and toiletries are already successful, like the children's wear.

4   **C:** *There's a flight for only $550 but it takes forever. That's via Los Angeles on the 15th.*
A: It costs $650 to fly via New York.
C: It costs $700 to fly via Hong Kong.

5   **B:** *Since 2001, when things were really bad, there has been a steady, if slow, improvement.*

6   **B:** *... I thought it would be simpler to hire a coach and pick them up altogether.*
A: Peter thought about getting the delegates to take taxis but decided against it.
C: Jean asks if Peter is taking the company car and Peter explains that there are too many people to do that.

7   **A:** *... there's something on your chair. Yes, here they are.*
B: The man thinks they are on his desk but he is mistaken.
C: Sue suggests that they might be in the filing cabinet before she see them on the chair.

8   **C:** *Eight altogether.*
A: There are six chairs there at the moment.
B: The woman thinks that they need seven chairs, but she has forgotten about the man who is coming to give the design brief.

p.60   LISTENING   Part 2

9   3: *So another three, at least, I think.* (line 11)
Not 5. There are five programmers at the moment but they need more.

10 $60,000: *let's say $60,000 over 6 months.* (lines 12–13)

11 $35,000: *so $35,000 by the end of stage two.* (line 19)
Not $5,000. That is the cost per month, not the cost for stage two.

12   4: *We'll need to have PCs for the three new programmers and one for the manager.* (lines 22–23)

13   1: *but basically we need a new photocopier.* (lines 26–27)

14 $50,000: *We're probably looking at $50,000 max for that lot plus the staffing costs.* (lines 29–30)

15   15%: *That's a significant increase in the agreed budget – about 15%, I think.* (lines 30–31)

FURTHER PRACTICE AND GUIDANCE (p.61)

A Detailed Study

1   1   two
       2   a project

2   **(10)** price
       (11) price
       (12) number
       (13) number
       (15) number

3   2   5 (programmers)
       3   3 (programmers)
       4   $60,000
       5   6 (months)
       7   $35,000
       8   2 (stage)
      10   1
      11   $50,000
      12   15%

p.62   LISTENING   Part 3

16   September 9th, 9/9: *Three years ago today (exactly – it was September 9th).* (lines 3–5)

17   old-fashioned: *They thought they were old-fashioned.* (lines 8–9)

18   interviews: *and held face-to-face interviews with another 10,000 of them who were visiting our stores.* (lines 19–21)

19   room: *A well-lit, spacious store and plenty of room to see the merchandise.* (lines 23–24)

20   sizes: *They wanted the clothes displayed well and available in all sizes.* (lines 24–26)

21 doors: *For example, there are automatic doors in every one of them.* (lines 30–31)

22 prices: *In some cases we had to lower our prices.* (lines 38–39)

FURTHER PRACTICE AND GUIDANCE (p.63)

A Detailed Study

1 1 chief executive, retail stores
   2 shareholders
   3 company

2 1 wrong
   2 do
   3 did we find out
   4 What changes did we make

3 16 noun (a date)
   17 adjective
   18 noun (something they did with customers)
   19 noun (something that would be good for the store)
   20 noun (colour or size)
   21 noun (something that is automatic, e.g. doors, windows)
   22 noun

p.64–65   LISTENING   Part 4

23 **C:** *And you are dressed today in an expensive looking suit – more like a banker. Somehow you are not my idea of a man who is an expert in aerosols!* (lines 11–14)
A: Philippe asks if the interviewer expected him to be wearing jeans and sunglasses.
B: The interviewer says Philippe Salenbier is a relatively young man but does not suggest that he is too young for the job.

24 **A:** *We are expanding the company and developing our product range. It's my goal this year to double the work force.* (lines 26–29)
B: They are planning to sell direct to supermarkets. This is part of the expansion plan. It is not Philippe's main aim.
C: They have already produced a new design for aerosols. This is part of the expansion plan. It is not Philippe's main aim.

25 **B:** *Well, people know we offer better salaries than other similar companies.* (lines 43–44)
A: Although the company is located in a beautiful part of France, it is isolated. It is difficult to find staff to move there.
C: One of the reasons that the salaries are higher is that the company does not offer company cars to its employees.

26 **A:** *We think a longer-term solution is to train and develop the staff we already have.* (lines 56–58)
B: Philippe believes the problem is a temporary one, not that the solution is to employ temporary staff.
C: Philippe says that offering generous relocation packages has not helped them in the past.

27 **B:** *Indeed. Economic growth, in particular. Turnover is up 6% and sales have increased by 25% in the first six months of this year.* (lines 62–65)
A: Philippe says that they do not yet have a complete range of products on the shelves.
C: Philippe says *we haven't lost out to our rivals.* He doesn't say that they have collapsed.

28 **C:** *Our customers – big high-street retailers mostly – demand cheaper and cheaper products.* (lines 73–75)
A: They get their raw ingredients from the Far East. They are not looking for new markets there.
B: Philippe says *it is almost impossible to get hold of certain ingredients in Europe …* He does not talk about cost.

29 **C:** *We have to make sure that we don't upset our customers, so we store extra stocks of popular products.* (lines 83–86)
A: Philippe says that deliveries can be held up. He doesn't say that they charge for them.
B: He doesn't say anything about the quality of the ingredients. He says that customers like the sound of ingredients coming from faraway places.

30 **B:** *We are introducing a range of aerosols for the home and garden which should sell well at any time of year.* (lines 102–105)
A + C: He says that they sell more expensive items at Christmas. He does not talk about reducing prices.

SPEAKING

FURTHER PRACTICE AND GUIDANCE (p.67–68)

A Detailed Study

1 **Location:** B, F, I
   Facilities: A, D, G
   Cost: C, E, H

2 **Advertising:** 1 D   2 B   3 F
   Quality: 1 E   2 A   3 C
   Delivery: 1 Make sure you have sufficient stocks.
   2 Don't forget to pack things carefully.
   3 It's vital to check dates for despatch.

TEST THREE

1   A: *You must not take documents out of the library without the permission of the librarian.* This means you must ask (permission) if you want to take documents out.
B: You are allowed to take documents out of the filing room but you must ask permission first.
C: The librarian does not need permission, he/she gives permission.

2   C: The advertisement says *Situated near the ferry terminal.*
A: There is no mention of how you get to the terminal.
B: A cleaning service means you can get your car cleaned. To service your car is to check its mechanical function.

3   B: The notice says *use public car park in Bewick Road.*
A: To get to Bewick Road, you turn left at the end of the building.
C: We are not told if the car park is behind the building.

4   A: The note says *they never received Invoice ER213.*
B: His company will receive, not issue, the invoice.
C: He needs to talk to Marissa, not Carmina.

5   C: You get the discount if you *pay your bill* in less than thirty days after you receive the goods.
A: There is no mention of when you receive the goods.
B: You are going to receive, not deliver the goods.

6   D: This is where she keeps overseas distributors' contact details.

7   G: This is where she keeps correspondence, i.e. letters sent and received.

8   E: *Similar products on the market* are those produced by competitors.

9   A: This is where she keeps back (or past) issues of the newsletters.

10 F: *Suppliers* are companies who supply goods and services to this company.

11 B: The phrase *Responses to the TV advertisement remained steady over the four months* could apply to B and H, but it was B where responses to the magazine advertisement *continued to grow steadily.*

12 F: The magazine advertisement did better than the TV advertisement throughout for B, E and F, but it is in F that the TV *advertisement gradually picked up well, particularly in April.*

13 H: The advertisements did *equally well* in A and H but it is in H that *responses to the magazine advertisement began to fall off towards the end of the period.*

14 C: C and D both show a lot of variation, but it is C where the magazine advertisement started and finished badly, while the TV advertisement did badly in the middle months.

15 A: The TV advertisement is *slightly ahead of the magazine advertisement* in A and G, but it is in A that *both tailed off in April* (*tailed off* means *went down*).

16 C: The administrator will work in the central office at national headquarters (lines 4–5) but the text does not say anything about the administrator having his/her own office.

17 B: The text says that the administrator will *be co-ordinating staff recruitment and appointment procedures* (lines 7–8) as part of his/her job of *providing … support services to the Programme Manager.* (line 6)

18 C: There is no reference to working without supervision (on your own).

19 B: The advertisement says *please do not send CVs at this stage* (lines 13–14). The phrase *at this stage* refers to when they apply for the form.

20 A: The advertisement says that there is a *24-hour answerphone.* (line 14)

21 A: The *Closing date for applications* is the last date that the applications will be accepted.

22 C: The advertisement says that emails must be addressed to Melanie Slim (line 15) but it does not say whether she will be an interviewer.

23 B: The key sentence is *If it is just a matter of changing or exchanging goods, the sales assistant can deal with it.* (lines 4–5)
A: This would be dealt with by *a Supervisor or Customer Services.* (line 7)
C: This would be dealt with by *someone higher up, such as the Store Manager.* (line 10)

24 A: The key phrase is *the customer refuses to listen or to accept the offered solution* (lines 8–9). This is when the Store Manager or Head Office would be involved.

B There is nothing in the text about overcharging the customer.
C The text refers to *staff rudeness* (line 6), not customer rudeness.

25 A: The key section is *they know that not all their goods are going to be perfect. They accept, therefore, that most (if not all) customer complaints are justified.* (lines 13–15)
B: This may be true in real life but the text does not say this.
C: There is nothing in the text about the percentage of goods returned.

26 C: The key sentence is *But if the store listens politely, checks the problem, and then offers a replacement or a refund, with an apology if needed, the customer will remain loyal.* (lines 19–21)
A: The store should listen to all complaints but the text does not say that the store should always agree with the complaint.
B: It is not the customers but the complaints that are referred to Head Office.

27 C: The key phrase is *many retailers have cut running costs by employing fewer staff.* (lines 25–26)
A: This is mentioned in the text but it is not the reason why it takes so long to get served.
B: The text says *there simply aren't enough sales assistants or staff at the checkout desks* (lines 26–27), so it is the shortage staff, not checkout desks that causes the problem.

28 A: The key phrase is *the more likely explanation is that people are readier to complain nowadays.* (lines 29–30)
B: This is wrong: the word *generation* (line 31) does not refer to the age of the customers.
C: This is not true: earlier parts of the text say that stores generally **do** listen more to their customers.

FURTHER PRACTICE AND GUIDANCE (p.80)

A Detailed Study

1 1 True: *Big companies have a special department to deal with customer complaints.* (line 1)
2 False: *if the matter still cannot be solved, which is usually because the customer refuses to listen or to accept the offered solution, it is referred to someone higher up, such as the Store Manager.* (lines 8–10)
3 False: *If it is just a matter of changing or exchanging goods, the sales assistant can deal with it.* (lines 4–5)
4 True: *That customer will not come back.* (lines 18–19)
5 True: *customer complaints are increasing.* (line 22)

6 False: *The commonest complaint is about staff who are unhelpful, usually because they know little about the product they are selling.* (lines 23–24) Being unhelpful is not the same as being impolite.
7 True: *The second thing that makes customers angry is having to wait too long to be served.* (lines 24–25)
8 True: *Citizens' Charters, telling people what they can expect and what to do if they are dissatisfied, have produced a generation of customers who know their rights and not afraid to demand them.* (lines 30–32)

2 23 *On the spot* means at the place and the moment where the customer makes the purchase. The person dealing with the customer is usually a sales assistant.
24 The more complicated cases include: damaged goods, a request for a refund or complaints about staff rudeness.
25 *Chain stores* are big companies that have branches in all the major towns. They usually accept that things will sometimes go wrong, so most complaints are justified.
26 The best way is to accept that things can go wrong, deal with the problem by listening carefully, checking the facts and then offering a replacement or a refund, and an apology if needed.
27 They are unhelpful because they don't know enough about the products they are selling, i.e., they cannot answer the customer's questions about the product.
28 Citizens' Charters have helped to make customers aware of their rights and to encourage them to complain about poor service or goods.

p.81 READING Part 6

29 A: *This is why* means *This is the reason why.* Compare the use of *why* and *because* in the following sentences:
*Some people eat too much **because** they are unhappy.*
*Joe is unhappy: that's **why** he eats too much.*
***Why** does Joe eat too much? It's **because** he is unhappy.*

30 C: The plural pronoun *their* goes with the plural noun *companies.*

31 B: *Who* refers to people and is used on its own. *Which* could only be used with a noun here, for example: ***which** people, **which** employees.*

32 C: The fixed expression is *for example.*

33 C: *the manager may not need to use English* means *it is possible that he needs to use English but equally possible that he doesn't need to use English.*

34 A: The fixed expression is *to deal **with***.

35 C: The fixed expression is ***on** the other hand*.

36 C: You can use *each* on its own, as it is here. You could also say *each one*. You cannot use *every* without a following noun or pronoun, that is, you would have to say *every one*. *Either* refers to a choice of two, so it would not make sense here.

37 B: The text describes a general situation so the present simple is used: *employees **use** English all the time; a manager and a waiter **need** … ; many people **want** to learn.*

38 C: *such employees* means *employees like the ones we just mentioned*, those who only need a reading knowledge of English.

39 A: The fixed expression is ***take** into account*. Companies should also give some importance to the wishes of their employees.

40 A: *see it as a passport* means they believe that English will help them to get a better job in the future.

p.83   READING   Part 7

41 OTTIMO BAKERIES
This is the new supplier. MAMMO was the old supplier.

42 MARIA SPEZZINI
Hers is the name on the OTTIMO leaflet.

43 OWNER (accept PROP)
Prop. on the Ottimo leaflet is short for *proprietor*, another word for owner.

44 01023 565715
This is the phone number for orders. 01023 565704 is for other inquiries.

45 15% DISCOUNT
This is the discount that Ottimo have agreed with Graziella. The normal discount is 10%

p.84   WRITING   Part 1

46 Model answer

> Thank you for the invitation to attend the AGM, which I accept with pleasure. I shall travel by train, arriving in Madrid at 17:50 hours on the 15th. Could you please arrange accommodation for me?

(35 words)

The email covers all the points:
- you have accepted the invitation: *Thank you for the invitation.*
- you have given travel details: *I shall travel by train, arriving in Madrid at 17:50 hours on the 15th.*
- you have requested help with accommodation: *Could you please arrange accommodation for me?*

p.85   WRITING   Part 2

47 Model answer

> Dear Ms Starling
>
> Thank you for your letter of 20th January offering me the post, which I am happy to accept.
>
> Unfortunately, I cannot start until 1st May because I have to give three months' notice to my present employer.
>
> You offer a starting salary of £42,000, but I have many years' experience, so I think I should start at £45,000.
>
> Could you give me details of the other conditions you refer to, in particular the company pension scheme and holiday entitlement?

(79 words)

The letter covers all the points:
- you have thanked her: *Thank you for your letter of …*
- you have accepted: *which I am happy to accept.*
- you have given a reason why you cannot start until May: *because I have to give three months' notice.*
- you have asked for details about other conditions: *Could you give me details of the other conditions you refer to.*

FURTHER PRACTICE AND GUIDANCE (p.86)

Follow up Activity

Letter from Person A (informal)
Dear Anne
I hear you're looking for a Sales Rep. I'm out of work at the moment, and just can't wait to get another rep's job.
I've had lots of sales experience with three different electronic companies. So I think I might be just the person you are looking for.
The basic salary you are offering seems a bit low, so can you please give me some idea how much I might earn in commission?
Hope to hear from you soon.
Yours

Letter from Person B (formal)

Dear Ms Freeman

I understand that your company is looking for a Sales Representative. My current status is unemployed, and I am seeking a suitable position in sales.

My experience includes work in the field of electronics. Therefore, I feel that I am a strong candidate for the post.

I would be grateful if you could give me some idea of the level of commission I might expect to earn.

May I thank you in advance for your kind attention.

Yours sincerely

Note on paragraphing:

It is easier for the person reading your letter if you start a new paragraph for each main idea. In the letter the main ideas are:

1 Opening paragraph: your present situation and interest in the job advertised.
2 Why you think you are suitable for the job.
3 Asking about salary and commission.
4 Closing sentence.

p.87–88   LISTENING   Part 1

1 **A:** *Yes, instead of the plain colours we have now – you know, orange for orange juice, green for apple juice …*
B: The woman suggests that the carton will look better if it is white with pictures of fruit on it.
C: At the moment the carton is a plain colour but has no pictures of fruit on it.

2 **B:** *… and then stopping production altogether a week later.*
On the eighteenth?
Yes.
A: They are slowing things down by the tenth but not stopping production altogether.
C: They are closing before the end of the month.

3 **A:** *Electrical goods have sold very well this month. That's good … As you know, May wasn't great and April was even worse.*

4 **A:** *Could you tell him I can't see him today.*
B: He can't see him at all today.
C: He will telephone him but not see him tomorrow.

5 **B:** *I think we should write to the chief executive and complain.*
A: There was a meeting with the manager last year but things did not improve.
C: There is no suggestion that staff should be involved.

6 **B:** *Ah, but soft drinks are doing even better.*
A: It's been a good week for cakes and biscuits but they are not selling better than soft drinks.
C: Frozen foods sold best last week.

7 **B:** *The ink is awfully faint.* and *I forgot to order a new ink cartridge, I'm afraid.*
A: The woman suggests writing the envelopes by hand but they haven't run out of them.
C: The quality of the printing is poor, not the labels.

8 **C:** *Says he'll see you at the restaurant.*
A: Mr Royal says he is about to leave his hotel.
B: The woman asks the man to look after the office while she goes out to the restaurant.

p.89   LISTENING   Part 2

9 Barber: *No. It's Barber. B-A-R-B-E-R.* (line 3)
Not 'Barr'. Martin says *Is that Miss Barr?* and Rebecca corrects him.
No. It's Barber. B-A-R-B-E-R.

10 1st December: *When is it due exactly?*
On the 1st December. (lines 10–11)
Not November. Rebecca says *Oh, of course, we're in November now.*

11 One million pounds or £1,000,000: *Your present cover is for one million pounds.* (lines 15–16)
Not £10,000 as she thinks: *What am I covered for at the moment? About ten thousand, isn't it?*

12 A hundred and seventeen pounds sixty or £117.60: *The annual fee is £117.60.* (line 18)
Not £9.80 as that is what she pays each month.

13 Nine pounds eighty or £9.80: *you pay off at £9.80 a month.* (lines 18–19)
Not £11. That is what she would pay if she paid in ten instalments: *or if, you prefer, in ten equal instalments of £11.*

14 One hundred and forty-six pounds or £146: *We have a special offer of £146 for two million.* (lines 25–26)
Not £200. That is for cover of five million: *There is another offer going of £200 for five million.*

15 JR 56782: *It's JR 56782 isn't it?* (line 33)
Not 01449 34. That is her telephone number: *My telephone number? It's 01449 34 …*

p.90   LISTENING   Part 3

16 The second week of August, 9th to 15th August: *At the moment there are still places left in the second week of August, so that's the 9th to the 15th.* (lines 8–10)

17 accommodation: *sounds expensive but it does include all your accommodation but not your food or travel.* (lines 11–13)

18 inflation: *In fact, there will be talks on familiar subjects such as 'SWOT analysis' and the 'effects of inflation'.* (lines 19–21)

19 Ford Motors: *there will be visits to the Bank of England in London and Ford motors in Dagenham.* (lines 30–31)

20 stock exchange: *they are hoping to invite someone from the stock exchange.* (lines 27–28)

21 a certificate: *At the end of the course there will be the usual farewell dinner where you'll be presented with a certificate if you've passed.* (lines 34–37)

22 50% refund: *the top student, that's the one who does best in the test at the end, will actually get a refund of 50% off the total cost of the course.* (lines 39–42)

p.91–92 LISTENING Part 4

23 **B:** *More and more people are either not finding or giving up permanent, full-time jobs.* (lines 7–8)
A: She has seen a change in work patterns not an increase in unemployment.
C: She says people are giving up jobs but not being made redundant.

24 **A:** *It is true that many companies no longer offer as many permanent posts as they used to.* (lines 11–13)
B: Companies are not offering so many long-term contracts not job contracts.
C: She mentions only that there are fewer permanent posts and that consequently these positions sometimes receive higher salaries.

25 **C:** *Well, it seems to be the case, doesn't it, that many firms offer a lot more part-time jobs as well?*
Yes. That is certainly a trend we are noticing, especially in certain sectors such as catering and retail.
(lines 19–24)
A: Part-time work used to mainly be at weekends and holidays but this is no longer the case.
B: This trend has been noticed amongst large retailers not all businesses.

26 **C:** *I can remember in the 1990s when I was starting up the business, I used to work 70 or 80 hours a week.*
(line 39–41)
A: She worked for 70 or 80 hours a week not in the 1970s.
B: As for A but not in the 1980s.

27 **B:** *I probably work better and I'm sure I'm more productive in the hours I do work. We call it 'working smart'.* (lines 49–51)
A: She has been self-employed since the 1990s when she was working long hours.
C: There is no indication that she doesn't care as much, only that she no longer wants to work so hard.

28 **A:** *The trouble is many people still think that part-time jobs or even temporary jobs are not 'real' jobs. That is rubbish.* (lines 58–61)
B: She believes that it is probably not possible for everyone to have a job. *It's also unrealistic because there aren't, as I said at the beginning, enough of those sorts of jobs to go round.*
C: She believes that many people don't want to work full-time. *All these people are choosing to work part-time.*

29 **A:** *Since 1995 total numbers have gone up by 5% …* (lines 74–75)
B: It is the over 40s where it has risen by 18%. … *but the rise for people over the age of 40 is 18% …*
C: It is the over 50s where the rise is 22% … *and it's 22% for the over 50s.*

30 **B:** *Interestingly, a significant number of mature people in their 50s are taking on part-time work to finance their return to education.* (lines 85–88)
A: Unemployment has increased amongst the over 40s, and they are not choosing to finance their education by working part-time.
C: More mothers are returning to work but not necessarily to finance their education.

FURTHER PRACTICE AND GUIDANCE (p.93–94)

A Detailed Study

1 1, 3, 4, 7 This is because these statements reflect in some way what is said in the question stem. The stem is the part of the multiple choice question at the beginning. It does not include the options A, B and C. Read through the question stems again and check this for yourself.

2 1 She is a consultant to a government department.
 2 She studies the way we work.
 3 They can do this because they don't have to employ staff on long-term contracts.
 4 No
 5 They employ a lot of part-time workers.
 6 She wanted to (and needed to as she was setting up her own business).
 7 A 'real' job is one that is permanent and full-time.
 8 They are working part-time to pay for their education.

Further Study

See answers to 25–28 above.

SPEAKING

FURTHER PRACTICE AND GUIDANCE (p.97)

A Detailed Study

1 1 F 2 C 3 D 4 E 5 B 6 A
2 1 H 2 D 3 A 4 H 5 A 6 D
 7 D 8 H 9 A

TEST FOUR

p.98–99   READING   Part 1

1 **B:** *your Supervisor… will call in the Technical Department if necessary.*
A: Clerical staff are told to *advise your Supervisor*.
C: It is the supervisor, not the member of the clerical staff, who will deal with the technical department

2 **C:** There are 2,100 per pack. There are 100 sheets per pack and each sheet has 21 labels.

3 **C:** The head office is in San Diego. 858 300 4000 is the telephone number, 858 300 4011 is the fax number.

4 **A:** The question *Have you spoken to Annie yet?* means that Bill should now phone Annie.
B: Sarah has forgotten to phone Annie, not Bill.
C: Sarah is asking if Bill has phoned Annie, not the other way around.

5 **B:** The advertisement says *express delivery, $25 surcharge on all packages*.
A: It says *orders over $75.00 free*. Orders worth less are *charged at normal postal rates*.
C: The company delivers *within country only*, so there are no overseas deliveries.

p.100–101   READING   Part 2

6 **H:** You use this to get cash for small purchases.

7 **B:** You use this form to order such things as stationery.

8 **G:** You use this form to reclaim money of your own which you have spent on company business.

9 **F:** When a supplier delivers goods to your company, you use this form to show you have received the goods

10 **E:** Most companies have a book (register) which is signed by visitors so that there is a record of the visitors' name and company, date and time when they arrived and departed, and who they came to see.

p.102–103   READING   Part 3

11 **G:** A and G both show falling sales *until August* but the phrase *sales, especially of electric mowers* points to G.

12 **B:** B shows the lowest sales overall for electric mowers, and the sale of petrol mowers peaks in July.

13 **A:** A and G both show falling sales, but the phrase *petrol mowers finally doing better than electric* points to A.

14 **C:** C, D and F all show improvement in electric mower sales but only C could be described as 'steady'. Both D and F show some ups and downs. Only C shows electric mowers *overtaking* petrol mowers in July. In D, electric sales were better than petrol in all months.

15 **F:** The phrase *roughly the same* could apply to A, F and G but only F shows a *slight dip* in May–July. The dip in G starts much earlier and finishes much later.

p.104–105   READING   Part 4

16 **C:** We know it took place a the National Press Office (line 6) but we do not know if this was in London.

17 **C:** There is no mention of this in the text.

18 **A:** They had to deal both with *scheduled visitors*, i.e., planned events, and also with *several unexpected incidents* (lines 17–18).

19 **C:** The text tells us that only a few companies offer training (lines 23–24), and that only one contestant performed well (lines 25–26) but this does not tell us if the **contestants** had had any training.

20 **A:** The phrase *each finalist in turn* (lines 27–28) mean that the finalists were interviewed separately.

21 **B:** Only the top two contestants were re-interviewed (lines 37–38).

22 **A:** The text refers to Ms Suzanne Burdette as *the successful contestant* (line 34).

p106–107   READING   Part 5

23 **C:** Some ideas were not used *mainly because of cost* (lines 5–6).
A + B: These may be true but they are not in the text.

24 **A:** The *better ventilation and air quality* (lines 5–6) would be the result of installing air conditioning.
B: The text refers to better lighting but lighting is not a machine.
C: The text refers to office layout but it does not say anything about personalizing work stations.

25 **C:** The text says *records show that time lost through illness and minor accidents went down* (lines 7–8).
A + B: These may be true but they are not in the text.

26 B: The text says she was *easily the best-qualified in terms of experience* (line 13).
A: This is not true. *The post was advertised nationally* (lines 10–11) and she reached the short list *not because she was our employee …* (line 13).
C: She got the diploma after she got the job (lines 14–15).

27 C: The text says she *introduced new rules for keeping work areas clean and tidy* (line 22).
A: She did not **introduce** safety clothing, she recommended **better** safety clothing (lines 19–20).
B: The *guards* (line 20) are not people but safety equipment such as covers to reduce the risk of accidents.

28 A: The text says *she has a wonderful ability to present her ideas in such a way that people come to believe that it was their idea in the first place!* (lines 25–27).
B + C: These may be true but they are not in the text.

p.108–109   READING   Part 6

29 A: You use *do* instead of repeating the main verb, for example: *I sometimes play football, and when I **do**, I always enjoy myself.*

30 A: The possessive adjective of *you* is *your: you will at some time suffer pain in **your** arms*. Similarly *they will suffer pain in **their** arms* and *she will suffer pain in **her** arms*.

31 B: *To do something **about** [a problem]* is a fixed expression. It means *to do something to solve the problem.*

32 C: The expanded phrase would be *which are like the ones …. As* and *such* would not fit here.

33 C: *To **keep** warm* is a fixed expression.

34 A: *To get **worse*** (like *to get better*) is a fixed expression. *Bad* does not fit because the problem is already bad, and it may get worse. *Worst* is the superlative form. There is no such expression as ~~get worst~~.

35 B: You use *try … -ing* when you have a problem and you are not sure how to solve it, so you try several things to see if they work, for example: *If you have hiccups, **try putting** a bunch of cold keys down your back.* This is different from *try to do.* You *try to do* something if you are not sure whether you can do it or not, for example: *I **tried to play** a didgeridoo and all I got was a rude noise.*

36 C: People who use a Maltron keyboard say *they no longer get any pain.* This is more or less the same as *they don't get any pain any more.* The word *less* would not fit. It is the comparative form of *little. Less* could be used in a sentence like *I suffer less pain than I used to,* thanks to the Maltron keyboard.

37 A: The word *cause* explains the reason **why** you have the problem. You cannot use *get* or *find* here.

38 C: This is a simple conditional: *if you get A, do B.*

39 A: *rather than* means *instead of.*

40 B: You use *spend* with expressions of time, for example: *to **spend a day** working in the garden.* Here, *too long* means *too much time.*

p.110–111   READING   Part 7

41 XENON P23-DE [PRINTING CALCULATOR]
Ms Booth' memo asks for *tax and euro functions.* Only this calculator has both.

42 TAX AND EURO FUNCTIONS

43 6 (SIX)
Ms Booth asks for one for each department and there are five departments. She also adds *plus one spare.*

44 COD [CASH ON DELIVERY]
Ms Booth specifies *COD* (cash on delivery).

45 WITHIN 3 (THREE) DAYS [OF RECEIPT OF ORDER]
She wants the goods to be *sent within three days* after the suppliers receive the order.

FURTHER PRACTICE AND GUIDANCE (p.112)

A Detailed Study

1 1 1 mistake: it should be *Sparks*, not *Sparkes*
   2 no mistakes
   3 1 mistake: it should be *Xenon*, not *Xennon*
   4 1 mistake: it should be *separator*, not *seperator*
   5 2 mistakes: it should be *FR620TER*, not *FR820LTEP*
   6 no mistakes

2 1 The departments need printing calculators because they have to keep careful financial records.
   2 Peter Sparks
   3 The Pi-E2005-Euro Printing Calculator has two-colour printing.
   4 The Denton Desktop calculator has an angled display for easy viewing and a thousands-separator.
   5 The company does not have an account with the supplier. In his memo, Mr Booth says *no need to open an account with these suppliers.*

6   The letters COD stand for *cash on delivery*, i.e., the person who delivers the goods will provide an invoice which you must pay immediately.

7   The expression *within three days* means *not more than three days* but it could be less than three days.

8   The word *receipt* comes from the verb *to receive*.

p.113   WRITING   Part 1

46   Model answer

> My dear Mizuki
>
> Sorry but I can't see you on Wednesday 24th after all, because my boss has arranged a board meeting on that day, which I must attend. Could we meet on the following Wednesday at 11 am? Please let me know.

(40 words)

The note covers all the points:

* you have apologized: *Sorry but I can't see you on Wednesday 24th after all.*
* you have explained why you cannot keep the appointment: *because my boss has arranged a board meeting… which I must attend.*
* you have suggested an alternative date and time: *on the following Wednesday at 11 am.*

FURTHER PRACTICE AND GUIDANCE (p.114)

A Detailed Study

1   A   An *appointment* is a meeting for something serious like a business meeting or seeing a doctor. A *date* is a casual meeting with a friend, relative or lover.

   B   *Colleagues* the people you work with. *Friends* are people you like to be with.

   C   A *firm* may have a main *branch* or headquarters in one town, and branches in several other towns. *Departments* are the sections within a single company, firm or branch of a company, for example, marketing, accounts, sales, etc.

   D   Adding the word *My* in front of *dear* makes it much more friendly or warm. We know, therefore, that you and Mizuki are not only colleagues but also that you know each other very well and like each other.

2   A   You could use any of them but *I am sorry that* is what most people would use. *I regret* is very formal and serious, not something you would write to a close colleague like Mizuki. *There's no way* is too informal and also suggests that you have strong feelings about the matter.

   B   You could use any of them. *The reason is* is the safest. *The thing is* is a bit too informal.

   C   You could use any of them. *I suggest* is probably what most people would use. *Why don't we* and *Do you think you could* are a little less formal, so they suitable for writing to Mizuki but not to someone higher up in the company, for example, a department head or boss.

   D   *Please let me know* and *I look forward to hearing from you* are good. *Love and kisses* is for writing to a lover or close family. *Yours faithfully* is how you finish off a letter which begin with *Dear Sir*.

p.115   WRITING   Part 2

47   Model answer

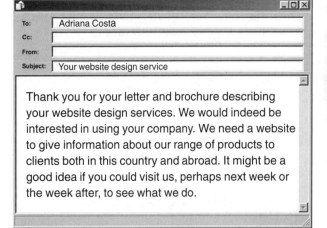

(76 words)

The email covers all the points:

* you have thanked her: *Thank you for your letter and brochure.*
* you have expressed an interest: *We would indeed be interested in using your company.*
* you have described what you would like: *We need a website to give information about our range of products.*
* you have suggested a meeting: *It might be a good idea if you could visit us*

p.116–118   LISTENING   Part 1

1   **C:** *The meeting doesn't start until two.*
A: The man thinks they should arrive by midday.
B: The man thinks they should leave by ten

2   **A:** *Is that the manager's car leaving the car park?*
… Yes.
B: The manager is going to meet the new chief executive for lunch.
C: The woman asks if the manager's personal assistant is with him in the car but Justin thinks it is his wife.

3   **A:** *My car wouldn't start so I had to come in by train.*
B: The woman asks if she can use the photocopier.
C: The woman had to come to work by train.

4   **C:** *… so I'm picking him up from his office in a few minutes.*
A: The man asks if she is taking Mr Wong to his hotel.
B: Mr Wong wants to meet at the restaurant.

5   **A:** *Our share price has fallen by ten euros since September.*

6   **C:** *We've given up motorbike production, though.*
A: The woman says the company is concentrating on producing luxury cars.
B: They have just had a large order for their trucks so they will go on producing them.

7   **B:** *In a surprising show of strength yesterday, ACME's shares went up by 37 cents to two dollars 49.*
A: Shares went up by 37 cents.
C: Profits of around 50 billion were forecast for the rest of the year.

8   **B:** *When you come out of the lift, turn right and it's the second room on your left at the end of the corridor.*

FURTHER PRACTICE AND GUIDANCE (p.119)

A Detailed Study

1   1   time
2   person
3   object
4   place
5   trend
6   object
7   price
8   place

2   1   arrangements
2   asking for information
3   asking permission
4   arrangements
5   money
6   products
7   money
8   giving directions

p.120   LISTENING   Part 2

9   July 1996: *Actually, our first store opened in July '96.* (line 13)
Not 1997. Alison asks if the supermarket set up in 1997 and Martin corrects her.

10   Gateshead (line 14)

11   350: *350, actually, in the North.* (line 22)
Not 200. Alison asks if they have over 200 stores and is told they have more.

12   6: *And we're due to open another six next year, in 2005.* (lines 24–25)
Not 5. The new stores will open in 2005.

13   40–60: *On average between forty and sixty in each store.* (lines 31–32)

14   1,500–2,000: *So, at present, between fifteen hundred and two thousand people.* (lines 32–33)

15   7%: *In fact, we now account for 7% of the food retail market.* (lines 37–38)
Not 2%. That refers to other sectors.

p.121   LISTENING   Part 3

16   dining rooms: *As you know, the refurbishment of the lounges and the private dining rooms is complete.* (lines 7–9)

17   weddings: *We have been particularly busy with weddings.* (lines 14–15)

18   chef: *Our chef and his team have continued to attract customers with exciting and innovative menus. Well done, Jamie.* (lines 19–21)

19   25%: *We've actually seen a 25% increase in non-residents coming to our restaurants this month already.* (lines 22–24)

20   director of sales: *I'd also like to welcome Jontje Lister who has recently joined us. Jontje is our new director of sales.* (lines 26–28)

21 London: *She has come from London where she has had many years of experience in the hospitality industry.* (lines 29–30)

22 dogs: *We have decided that as a country hotel group we will be making a point of welcoming dogs* (lines 33–34)

p.122–123   LISTENING   Part 4

23 **A:** The presenter says that in the past *the greatest challenge was to make a good speech. That was easy enough if you had someone good to write it for you.* (lines 7–10)
B: She says that all you had to do was *smile now and again* not 'a lot'.
C: She says that the *long, sometimes dull and boring speech to the shareholders is less important* these days

24 **C:** She says *it's a big mistake to say something that sounds like you've made notes first.* (lines 17–19)
A: She says if you are too prepared, you *may sound like you are reading out the brochure!*
B: She advises you not to *give too much detail*

25 **A:** She says that giving an interview is *more like a presentation.* (line 27)
B: She says *it may feel like you're having a conversation* but it isn't
C: What you say may *get reported back to the shareholders!* but it isn't therefore a report.

26 **B:** *Instead, stick to the headlines …* (lines 37–38)
A: You may be used to *giving your teams lots of reasons why certain decisions have been made?* but *Don't do that on camera*
C: She reminds you to be aware that you won't have much time but she doesn't tell you to monitor it.

27 **B:** She says you should *use the chance to tell thousands of people how good your company is and how they really need your products or skills.* (lines 44–47)
A: She refers to *all these warnings* she has given but stresses the positive side *it's not all bad news.*
C: She suggests that you *Make them want to interview you again* not that TV interviews are absolutely necessary.

28 **C:** She says *it's good to have an opening sentence which sends the message you want people to hear.* (lines 49–51)
A: She says *end the interview on a positive note if you can.*
B: She doesn't think politeness is a major factor *Don't just say 'It's nice to be here' or 'thank you for inviting me'*

29 **A:** She says *Then there are always those tricky questions. If a question comes up that you can't or don't want to answer, give yourself some time.* (lines 55–58)
B: She doesn't say that the questions are interesting only that you should **say** they are *Say 'Now that's an interesting question'*
C: She doesn't say there will be hidden questions only *If you do it badly it may sound like you are hiding something.*

30 **C:** She says *Don't relax until you are well away from the studio and driving home in your car.* (lines 66–68)
A: She says you shouldn't relax *Even if the light on top of the camera isn't on, take care.*
B: She advises you to *stay awake even after the interview has finished.*

SPEAKING

FURTHER PRACTICE AND GUIDANCE (p.126)

A Detailed Study

1   **Suggested Answers**
   1B don't like travelling very much anyway.
   2A they can help you understand how other countries do business.
   2B I think that people waste a lot of time and money on business trips.
   3A they think it is important to meet people they do business with face to face.
   3B are not necessary because they can talk to people on the phone and this can save them money.
4   visit countries I haven't been to yet. I think visiting new places is exciting.
5   face to face you can deal with problems more easily. I think you can understand each other

LISTENING SCRIPTS

TEST ONE   PART ONE

Example

Woman: Can you see what that sign says? Is it the entrance?
Man: No, it says 'exit'.
Woman: Well, we've got to park somewhere.
Man: Don't worry. I think that's the way in over there.
Woman: Thank goodness!

Question 1

Woman: James, I am sorry but I can't go to the cinema tonight.
James: Oh dear. Why's that?
Woman: I forgot that I've got to meet the directors at half-past six. I don't think I'll leave the office before half-past seven and the film starts at eight.
James: Never mind. We'll go another night.

Question 2

Man: Where did you say you're moving to, Natalie?
Natalie: Nowhere. I'm staying in Dublin but Head Office is moving to Belfast.
Man: Belfast? But isn't your company opening a new store in Cork?
Natalie: Yes but they've decided to make Belfast the administrative centre because we already have an office there.

Question 3

Woman: Yes, sir. Can I help you?
Herr Frank: You have some information for me? I heard an announcement, I think.
Woman: Are you Herr Frank, flying to Munich this afternoon?
Herr Frank: Yes, I am.
Woman: And have you checked in?
Herr Frank: Of course, my flight leaves very soon.
Woman: Good. You must go to gate seventeen immediately.
Herr Frank: Oh, which way is that?
Woman: It's over there, sir.

Question 4

Woman: Have you seen Mr Fleming, Karl? There's a call from the production line for him.
Karl: I think he's gone for lunch. He'll be back in an hour.

Woman: Oh dear. There's a problem with the car doors. They want him to come over. It's urgent.
Karl: Don't worry. I'll tell him. I'm going over to the canteen now.

Question 5

Man: So how is steel production at the moment?
Woman: Well, things are improving. Since April we've seen output increase from thirty to sixty thousand tonnes. That's good compared with two thousand and two.
Man: Yes, at the end of last year it was down to twenty thousand tonnes, wasn't it?

Question 6

Woman: And now to the currency report. The euro is looking stronger again. In fact, some experts are saying we could see one dollar equal to one euro by the end of the year. But, for the moment, the exchange rate is up from point nine three at the end of trading yesterday to point nine seven today. Of course, anything could happen tomorrow. Meanwhile, sterling is weakening against the dollar. The pound is now worth …

Question 7

Woman: Hello, Spaulls Printing Services.
Man: Hi there. Yes. It's about the computer you left with us. We've had it thoroughly checked over and it's ready for you to collect.
Woman: Do you mean the flat screen monitor?
Man: Sorry, madam. You're quite right. I was looking at the wrong print-out. Yes, it's ready for you.
Woman: Great. I'll come over for it this afternoon.

Question 8

Woman: Am I through to Mr Firth?
Operator: No, madam. It's the operator speaking.
Woman: Oh dear. I want to speak to someone who knows about a damaged parcel I received.
Operator: That'll be Customer Services.
Woman: Is Mr Firth the manager?
Operator: No, madam, but I'm sure there'll be someone there to help you.
Woman: All right then.

TEST ONE PART TWO

Irina:	John, can I go through the interview programme with you?
John:	Of course, Irina. There are seven of them, aren't there?
5 **Irina:**	Not now. One's dropped out.
John:	Six then, fine. When are they arriving?
Irina:	Nine-fifteen in reception – so be there by nine at the latest.
John:	OK. Then what?
10 **Irina:**	Interviews begin at ten, after coffee in the board room. I expect to spend about twenty minutes with each of them, so I should be through by twelve.
John:	What about the tests?
15 **Irina:**	In the board room. As they come out of their interviews, I want you take them to Nina. She'll sort them out.
John:	Who's Nina?
Irina:	Nina Conti, my new assistant. Haven't you met her yet?
20	
John:	Nina who?
Irina:	Conti, C-O-N-T-I. She's Italian.
John:	Great! Look forward to meeting her.
Irina:	Then there's lunch. That'll be in the canteen between one and two-thirty. Give the chef a ring at twelve-thirty to remind him you're coming.
25	
John:	OK. Is Nina coming for lunch?
Irina:	John!
30 **John:**	Sorry!
Irina:	Finally, make sure you pay them their travelling expenses. I know one person had to pay over a hundred pounds for a rail ticket. Use petty cash. I've already had a word with Accounts about it.
35	
John:	How much will I need?
Irina:	Three hundred pounds should cover it, but make sure they sign for everything and collect the receipts.
40 **John:**	No problem, boss.

TEST ONE PART THREE

Man: My family has been in agriculture since the nineteen-twenties. Being a farmer is a hard life but I loved it. Anyway, I was getting older and my son was studying to be a doctor and my daughter wasn't interested in taking over the farm. So I started Agriproducts in 1994, after nearly twenty years working on the land. I knew how difficult it was to market products successfully. My company buys directly from farmers and markets and sells everything for them. We help them decide what to grow and find out if there is a market for it or if we can create a market for it. I didn't know much about dairy products, so in the first five years we concentrated on finding markets for meat and animal feeds.

My first location was in the middle of the countryside. We had plenty of space – land was still cheap. I had the time and the money to build things up slowly. The only major disadvantage was we were not very near to airports or railways. However, we were only thirty miles from the motorway. But in 2001 we moved to a large site just outside London. That was when we started to export our products overseas. In fact, the first country we exported to was Spain. By the end of the year we were exporting a thousand tonnes of feed and that grew to two thousand in 2002. Since then we have established markets in Germany, Portugal and Italy.

Our next major project is to create a new market for high-quality organic fruit and vegetables. It may seem strange for a UK company to be exporting things like that to southern Europe but although their oranges are great, I think our apples are better! Still, we're going to concentrate on the home market first and test the water. Growing organically is very trendy but it is definitely more expensive.

TEST ONE   PART FOUR

Karen: I first met Sharon when she was giving me a manicure. While she was making a very good job of my nails, she was also chatting away to me. As she smiled and talked I
5 noticed that she was also looking round the salon and, from time to time, speaking to the receptionist or looking to see what the other beauticians were doing. I realized that she was the manager and, from what I
10 could see, a very good manager. Someone who was able to do ten things at once and still appear cheerful and calm. Sharon, I've invited you here today to find out how you do it.

15 **Sharon:** Thank you, Karen. I'm pleased to be here. Yes, I do think I'm a good manager but I think that's for two reasons, really. First of all, I like people and I like being with people and secondly, I like to know how
20 people are getting on together. I watch everybody all the time. I don't think they realize it because I don't make a big thing of it. I just keep my eyes and ears open.

Karen: And how did you get to be a manager?
25 **Sharon:** Well, it wasn't what I wanted to be. I was working as a manicurist in a small salon in a department store. It helped pay for my secretarial course I was doing in the evenings. My manager was off sick for a
30 few months and when she decided not to come back, the directors asked me to take over. It was more money, so I agreed.

Karen: You must have been good. But what you're doing now is a bit different. You manage
35 the salon for your husband, do you?

Sharon: Well he put some money into it and he does the accounts but the salon is in my name. In fact, most of the money was left to me by my father.

40 **Karen:** So how long have you been open?

Sharon: We bought the premises eighteen months ago. It was February and freezing cold! We were due to open in January but we had a fire in the basement. We opened properly in
45 April – so it's been about six months.

Karen: And it's going well?

Sharon: Incredibly well. I've taken on three assistants – so there's five of us now, including the receptionist – and it looks like
50 we are going to expand even further. I think we'll need two more staff by Christmas. We have a lot of regular clients and that's very important in this line of business. You need to have good relationships with your
55 customers. They like to feel comfortable and that you know all about them.

Karen: Why is that?

Sharon: I think it's because it's a very personal service. I mean, we see our customers when they are not looking their best. You know
60 they come in thinking they look terrible. They need to know you will be kind and say the right thing. And make them feel OK about spending time and money on themselves, too.
65

Karen: So in a way what you are doing is a bit like going to see a doctor.

Sharon: Well, yes, in a way. I can make them feel better because they look better. I think I have time to give them, 'though. If they
70 come in for a facial or a massage, that's at least an hour. And they like to talk about their problems. Sometimes you get their whole life stories! Of course, all I do is listen.
75

TEST TWO   PART ONE

Example

Woman: Can you see what that sign says? Is it the entrance?
Man: No, it says 'exit'.
Woman: Well, we've got to park somewhere.
Man: Don't worry. I think that's the way in over there.
Woman: Thank goodness!

Question 1

Woman: Has the stationery order arrived yet? We're out of photocopying paper.
Man: Oh dear. I only ordered it on Friday.
Woman: Friday! We usually order on a Thursday so that it's here by Monday.
Man: Sorry. I'll remember in future.
Woman: Never mind. See if you can get some from reception. They usually have some spare.
Man: OK.

Question 2

Man: Have you met Chris Sharp, our new project manager, yet?
Woman: No, how do you do?
Man: Chris joined J P Engineering last month. You were with Ashlings before that, weren't you, Chris?
Chris Well, no, actually. I was working for a government department. I was offered a job with Ashlings last year but decided to come here.
Woman: So, what do you think of the project so far …?

Question 3

Man: As you know, this year we have improved our sales figures and I want to continue to increase profitability. Our new range of children's wear is very successful, as are our own brands of perfume and other toiletries. But I want to do something new. So I've decided to open our first food hall.

Question 4

Woman: Hi there. I want to book a flight to Sydney, next week.
Man: I'll just see what's available.
Woman: Thanks.
Man: There's a flight for only $550 but it takes forever. That's via Los Angeles on the 15th.
Woman: Nothing earlier?

Man: You can fly via New York on the 11th for $650 and there's a seat on the 10th for $700. That's a good one. That's with a 24-hour stopover in Hong Kong.
Woman: Anything cheaper via New York?
Man: No, I'm sorry.
Woman: OK. I'll take it.

Question 5

Woman: I believe I may have some good news to report at last. Since 2001, when things were really bad, there has been a steady, if slow, improvement. We're hoping that this will continue.
Now, to put a bit more detail on that: in January of this year we were encouraged to see that …

Question 6

Jean: How are the delegates getting to the conference hall, Peter? Are you taking the company car?
Peter: No, Jean. There are eighteen of them! I considered getting them to take taxis but then I thought it would be simpler to hire a coach and pick them up all together.
Jean: Good idea! I can just imagine how many would be late if they were all in separate cars.

Question 7

Man: Sue, is that you? I've done something really silly.
Sue: What's that?
Man: I've left my notes for the meeting in my room. They're on my desk, I think. Can you see?
Sue: No, your desk's clear. Could they still be in the filing cabinet? Wait a minute, there's something on your chair. Yes, here they are. Do you want me to bring them over?
Man: Please!

Question 8

Man: Have you got enough chairs? There's six here.
Woman: Let me see. There's the chairman, his PA, the other directors – four of them said they were coming – and me. So we need seven.
Man: What about that chap who's giving them a report on the design brief?
Woman: You're right. We'll need another two. Eight altogether.

TEST TWO   PART TWO

Paul:	Morning, Jade, Paul here. It's about the Potter project. We're four weeks behind schedule and I think that we're going to have to spend more time and more money if we want to put things right.
Jade:	Can you give me a bit more detail?
Paul:	For a start, we need more programmers – at least for the next few months.
Jade:	There are five of them at present, aren't there?
Paul:	Yes. So another three, at least, I think.
Jade:	Really? That would be … let's say $60,000 over six months.
Paul:	I also think we need someone in overall charge. I simply don't have the time.
Jade:	OK, calm down Paul. A dedicated project manager, you mean?
Paul:	Yes. And we'd have to pay at least $5,000 a month, so $35,000 by the end of stage two. And then there's the hardware …
Jade:	Go on.
Paul:	We'll need to have PCs for the new programmers and one for the manager. And the team are complaining about the photocopier. It's not up to the job. A scanner would help, but basically we need a new photocopier.
Jade:	I agree about those. We're probably looking at $50,000 max for that lot plus the staffing costs. That's a significant increase in the agreed budget – about 15%, I think. Never mind. Leave it with me and I'll see what I can do.

TEST TWO   PART THREE

Woman: Good afternoon everybody. It's good to see so many of you here today. I want to start by telling you that we got it wrong. Three years ago today (exactly – it was September 9th) it looked then as though we might have to close the business. We hadn't been listening to our customers and we thought they liked the clothes. They didn't. They thought they were old-fashioned. And we thought that we could charge high prices because we were quality. But that wasn't enough. We thought our stores were fine the way they were. They weren't. They were poorly designed and the lighting was not good. It made the clothes look unattractive.

So we decided to do something to save the company. We sent a mail-shot to 3,000 of our customers and held face-to-face interviews with another 10,000 of them who were visiting our stores.

We found out that they wanted several things. A well-lit, spacious store and plenty of room to see the merchandise. They wanted the clothes displayed well and available in all sizes. And they wanted quality but at the right price.

I am happy to say that in three years we have achieved a lot. Our stores have been redesigned. For example, there are automatic doors in every one of them. The lighting is bright but not harsh, and we've spent a lot of time on our displays and introduced a new range of clothes for all the family.

Most importantly, we decided that we must continue to offer quality but at a price people want to pay. In some cases we had to lower our prices. That simple. And I'm happy to say the plan is working. Our sales figures are significantly up on last year.

Only time will tell if we can continue to get it right but I am confident that we will and I will continue to work at listening to our customers.

TEST TWO   PART FOUR

Rachel: Today I am talking to Philippe Salenbier who runs Vaporette International. Vaporette is a multi-national company which manufactures aerosol sprays that are used in everything from shaving foam to furniture polish. Philippe, if I may say so, you are a relatively young man ... forty-two, I believe?

Philippe: Yes, I am.

Rachel: And you are dressed today in an expensive looking suit – more like a banker. Somehow you are not my idea of a man who is an expert in aerosols!

Philippe: What did you expect? That I should come in jeans and a T-shirt with sun-glasses?

Rachel: Not exactly!

Philippe: I'm sorry to disappoint you, Rachel. But, you know, aerosols are very exciting. They are not just the thing you use to spray on your shaving foam!

Rachel: And I believe that there's a lot going on at Vaporette.

Philippe: Yes. We're expanding the company and developing our product range. It's my goal this year to double the work force. We have produced a completely new design of aerosol – it comes in a variety of shapes because the technology has changed. We are planning to have these new products on the shelves of your local supermarket in the next few months.

Rachel: And I see you are located in a very beautiful part of south-west France. It must be a wonderful place to live and work.

Philippe: But isolated. It has been difficult to find skilled staff to move here.

Rachel: What can you do about that?

Philippe: Well, people know we offer better salaries than other similar companies. We don't give away shares in the company or give our executives expensive company cars. I think most people today want a good salary. All the same, we have to do something about the lack of certain types of skilled staff.

Rachel: I imagine it's important to be given help with the cost of moving here.

Philippe: Actually, no. Offering generous relocation packages has not been very successful. We think a longer-term solution is to train and develop the staff we already have. I think the problem is a temporary one.

Rachel: I see. But you are still happy about the business in general?

Philippe: Indeed. Economic growth, in particular. Turnover is up 6% and sales have increased by 25% in the first six months of this year. We may not have our complete range on the shelves yet but next year ... And we haven't lost out to our rivals. We are still selling more cheaply and keeping our profitability.

Rachel: It's a competitive market price-wise out there ...

Philippe: It is. Our customers – big high-street retailers mostly – demand cheaper and cheaper products. We now get our 'raw ingredients', such as perfume, in the Far East. In fact, it's almost impossible to get hold of certain ingredients in Europe anymore.

Rachel: Is there a problem with importing from the Far East?

Philippe: Not really. Deliveries from the Far East can be held up sometimes. We have to make sure that we don't upset our customers, so we store extra stocks of popular products. We never have to disappoint a customer who may suddenly want an urgent order for something and we don't charge extra for offering this service. In fact, most of our customers like the sound of ingredients coming from faraway places.

Rachel: And with Christmas coming up you must be looking forward to increased sales ...

Philippe: It's the most important time of year for us. Our challenge is to increase sales at other times. We sell more expensive items at Christmas, so part of the solution is to focus on the less expensive items at other times. We're introducing a range of aerosols for the home and garden which should sell well at any time of year.

Rachel: Can you tell me a bit more about them ... ?

TEST THREE   PART ONE

Example

Woman: Can you see what that sign says? Is it the entrance?
Man: No, it says 'exit'.
Woman: Well, we've got to park somewhere.
Man: Don't worry. I think that's the way in over there.
Woman: Thank goodness!

Question 1

Woman: I've got an idea for the cartons.
Man: For the new range of fruit juices?
Woman: Yes, instead of the plain colours we have now – you know, orange for orange juice, green for apple juice ...
Man: Yes ...
Woman: I thought we could have pictures of fruit on them.
Man: So the orange carton will have oranges on, and so on.
Woman: Well, no. The carton will be white. What do you think?
Man: Yes, it could work ...

Question 2

Man: It's bad news, I'm afraid.
Woman: Oh dear. Are we going to close at the end of the month then?
Man: Worse. We are looking at slowing things down by the tenth and then stopping production altogether the following Friday.
Woman: On the eighteenth?
Man: Yes.
Woman: We'll have to tell everybody as soon as possible then.

Question 3

Man: Hi there, Malcolm. Have you seen the figures for this month? Some good news at last. Electrical goods have sold very well this month.
Malcolm: That's good. I know the company was getting quite worried about it. As you know, May wasn't great and April was even worse.
Man: That's right. Let's hope this trend continues.

Question 4

Frank: Good morning. It's Frank Lee speaking. Could I leave a message for Sam Singh, please?
Woman: Yes, of course.

Frank: Could you tell him I can't see him today. I'll call him tomorrow to rearrange things.
Woman: So you can't see him today but you'll meet him tomorrow?
Frank: No. I'll call him tomorrow. I can't see him.
Woman: OK. I'll pass that on.
Frank: Thanks. Bye.
Woman: Bye.

Question 5

Man: You know there's still not enough room in the car park for all the staff. I'm going to speak to the manager about it.
Woman: That won't do any good. Last year we had a meeting about it with the manager and things didn't improve. I think we should write to the chief executive and complain.
Man: The chief executive? Will he be interested?
Woman: Possibly.

Question 6

Man: So it's been a good week for confectionery and cakes and biscuits, I see.
Woman: Yes. Last week it was frozen foods that came out top.
Man: Ah, but soft drinks are doing even better. I think that must be because of the party season.
Woman: Yes, they are definitely our best-selling line this week.

Question 7

Woman: Oh dear, these labels look terrible. You can't really read the addresses at all. The ink is awfully faint.
Man: I see what you mean. I think it's my fault. I forgot to order a new ink cartridge, I'm afraid.
Woman: Never mind. Perhaps I'd better write these envelopes by hand.
Man: Don't worry, I'll go and see if I can get one from another department. I'll make sure it's on the stationery order for this week.

Question 8

Man: That was Mr Royal on the phone. He's leaving his hotel now. Says he'll see you at the restaurant. Shall I let him know you're on your way?
Woman: Don't worry. I'll call him on my mobile once I'm in the taxi. Can you look after things in the office?
Man: Sure, don't worry. You know everything will be fine.
Woman: OK. You can get me there if you need to.
Man: I know! Now, time to go or you'll be late!

TEST THREE   PART TWO

Rebecca: Hello. Rebecca Barber speaking

Justin: Is that Miss Barr?

Rebecca: No. It's Barber. B-A-R-B-E-R

Justin: I'm sorry, Miss Barber. My name is Justin
5 and I'm calling from PMG Insurance. I'm
calling to remind you that your
professional insurance policy is due for
renewal.

Rebecca: Oh, of course, we're in November now.
10 When is it due exactly?

Justin: On the 1st December. You may like to think
about increasing your cover.

Rebecca: What am I covered for at the moment?
About ten thousand, isn't it?

15 **Justin:** Your present cover is for one million
pounds.

Rebecca: And what does that cost me?

Justin: The annual fee is £117.60 which you pay off
at £9.80 a month or if, you prefer, in ten
20 equal instalments of £11 – that's a small
saving there. Then again, you might like to
consider increasing this to two million or
five million. As you may be aware, the
courts are awarding higher and higher
25 sums at the moment. We have a special
offer of £146 for two million. There is
another offer going of £200 for five million,
but perhaps you don't need to go that high.

Rebecca: I don't know. Seems like a lot of money.

30 **Justin:** Well, if you'd like to think about it … Just
call me back later with your scheme
number and I'll see what we can do for you.
It's JR 56782 isn't it?

Rebecca: My telephone number? It's 01449 34 …

35 **Justin:** No, your scheme number.

Woman: Oh yes, sorry! Let me see … it's JR – yes,
that's it. Thanks. I'll give it some thought.

Justin: In the mean time, you'll be receiving the
renewal forms in the post.

40 **Rebecca:** Thanks. Bye.

Justin: Goodbye, and thank you for your time.

TEST THREE   PART THREE

Man: Before you go, I'd like to tell you about the
business courses I'm involved in during the
summer in the UK. It will be a great
opportunity for you to improve your
5 English while you reinforce some of the
work you've been doing this year. Each
course lasts a week and is fairly intensive.
At the moment there are still places left in
the second week of August, so that's the 9th
10 to the 15th. The total cost, which I'll come to
in a minute, sounds expensive but it does
include all your accommodation, though
not your food or travel. During the week,
which is hard work but very interesting,
15 there are seminars on a variety of topics.
Now, before you say, 'Oh no, not all that
stuff again on communication and
customer care!', let me say this is different.
In fact, there will be talks on familiar
20 subjects such as 'SWOT analysis' and 'the
effects of inflation' but you'll be pleased to
hear that the people talking about these
things will be guest speakers from the real
world. At the moment I believe that
25 business guru Martin Porter will be coming
– he's from the airline sector – and I know
they are hoping to invite someone from the
stock exchange. I'll let you know more
about that later. Then, if you're interested,
30 there will be visits to the Bank of England in
London and Ford Motors in Dagenham.
Although I expect many of you might
prefer to go to the nightclubs and pubs of
old London town. At the end of the course
35 there will be the usual farewell dinner
where you'll be presented with a certificate
if you've passed and a slap on the back if
you haven't! And just to make you keener,
the top student, that's the one who does
40 best in the test at the end, will actually get a
refund of 50% off the total cost of the
course. Now that's worth having, isn't it?
So let me tell you a bit about the costs and
so on …

TEST THREE   PART FOUR

Howard: Helen James is a consultant to a government department and is currently looking at trends in employment and redundancy.

5 **Helen:** Good morning, Howard. Yes, what I am seeing at the moment is a change in work patterns. More and more people are either not finding or giving up permanent, full-time jobs. Others
10 simply can't get full-time work.

Howard: So there's more unemployment?

Helen: That's not what I'm looking at. It is true that many companies no longer offer as many permanent posts as they used to.
15 In fact, these days it doesn't make good business sense for most companies to take on staff on long-term contracts. But that often means that they can afford higher salaries.

20 **Howard:** Well it seems to be the case, doesn't it, that many firms offer a lot more part-time jobs as well.

Helen: Yes. That is certainly a trend we are noticing, especially in certain sectors
25 such as catering and retail.

Howard: But it's always been possible to get part-time work in shops and restaurants.

Helen: Yes it has, but we are seeing something different. Often those part-time jobs
30 were to cover for holidays or weekend work. Now we are seeing that some of the largest retailers employ nearly all their staff on the shop floor on a part-time basis.

35 **Howard:** Not the managers, though.

Helen: No, not usually at the top. But some of the middle managers are now part-time. And it works.

Howard: But surely that's a bad thing for society?
40 **Helen:** Is it? I can remember in the 1990s, when I was starting up the business, I used to work 70 or 80 hours a week. Sometimes more. It was what I wanted to do and I lived to work. The trouble was that I
45 thought that people who didn't work so many hours were not serious about their jobs.

Howard: You don't work so hard?

Helen: I don't work so many hours. I probably
50 work better and I'm sure I'm more productive in the hours I do work. We call it 'working smart'.

Howard: Yes, it sounds sensible. But for most people having a full-time, permanent
55 job is what's important, isn't it?

Helen: I don't think so. In fact, we have to change our opinions about the way we work and this *is* what I feel strongly about. The trouble is, many people still think that part-time jobs – or even 60 temporary jobs – are not 'real' jobs. That is rubbish. It's also unrealistic because there aren't, as I said at the beginning, enough of those sorts of jobs to go round. 65

Howard: So what do we do?

Helen: We have to start thinking about work in a different way. I think we must try to stop people thinking that if we are not working full-time or if we don't have a 70 permanent job then we are not serious workers.

Howard: Yes. And I believe that the total number of people in work has increased.

Helen: That's right. Since 1995 total numbers 75 have gone up by 5% but the rise for people over the age of 40 is 18% and it's 22% for the over 50s. Much of this increase amongst mature people is due to them taking on part-time work. 80

Howard: And I understand that the number of mothers returning to work after having a family is also increasing.

Helen: Yes, that's true. And all these groups may be deciding to find work that fits in 85 with their lives. Interestingly, a significant number of mature people in their 50s are taking on part-time work to finance their return to education. All these people are choosing to work part- 90 time.

Howard: So what we are looking at here is a complete change in …

TEST FOUR   PART ONE

Example

Woman: Can you see what that sign says? Is it the entrance?
Man: No, it says 'exit'.
Woman: Well, we've got to park somewhere.
Man: Don't worry. I think that's the way in over there.
Woman: Thank goodness!

Question 1

Man: I think we should leave by ten if we're to get there by midday, don't you?
Woman: Well, it doesn't matter too much. The meeting doesn't start until two. They're giving us lunch first. I've got a lot of work to do, so I don't want to leave right now.
Man: Oh, I suppose you're right. I could do some work but I don't really feel like it. I think I'll have another cup of coffee!

Question 2

Woman: Jason, come over here. Is that the manager's car leaving the car park? I thought we had a meeting with him.
Jason: Let's have a look. Yes. He's going to meet the new chief executive for lunch.
Woman: Oh dear. I must have made a mistake. Is that his PA in the car with him?
Jason: Oh no! He never takes her anywhere with him. Must be his wife. What meeting did you think you were having?

Question 3

Woman: Can I use your photocopier, Ken? The one in our office has got an enormous queue and I'm in a hurry to get this report out.
Ken: Sure. Why the hurry? I thought you were trying to slow down a bit.
Woman: I am, but I was late in today. My car wouldn't start so I had to come in by train.
Ken: Take a tip from me. Live near work so that you don't have to rely on public transport!

Question 4

Man: Are you taking Mr Wong to his hotel? I hear he's feeling really tired after his flight.
Woman: No. He said he wanted to meet at the restaurant, so I'm picking him up from his office in a few minutes. I expect he wants to get the meeting with the director out of the way first. Want a lift? There's going to be plenty of room. I'm taking the company car.
Man: Yes, please. That'd be great.

Question 5

Woman: What's the matter Shane? You look worried.
Shane: I'm trying to make sense of the share prices that have just come through.
Woman: Not good news then?
Shane: No. Our share price has fallen by ten euros since September. I think we may have to do something drastic.
Woman: Pity. Things were looking good before then. But then again, whose shares are doing well?

Question 6

Man: I hear you aren't producing any more vehicles this year.
Woman: Not quite! We've decided to concentrate on our luxury car range. The profit margins are so much higher. We've given up motorbike production, though.
Man: Shame. What about the large trucks? I thought they were doing well.
Woman: They are. We've just received a large order from Latvia, so we're keeping on with them.

Question 7

Woman: Good morning. Here is the business news. It was a slow start yesterday but prices ended up higher in some sectors. In a surprising show of strength, ACME's shares went up by 37 cents to two dollars 49. This was after an announcement that profits around the 50 billion mark are forecast for the new year. Good news for some but other companies did less well.

Question 8

Man: I've come for the directors' meeting. Is it in this building?
Woman: Let me see. Yes, it's in the board room.
Man: Where's that?
Woman: On the fourth floor. When you come out of the lift, turn right and it's the second room on your left at the end of the corridor.
Man: Thanks. I'll find it.

TEST FOUR   PART TWO

Alison:	Hello. Is that Freshfields, the supermarket chain?
Martin:	Yes. It's Martin Conran speaking. I'm the publicity manager.
Alison:	Great. I'm Alison Warner and I'm phoning from *The Caterer Magazine* because, as you know, we're doing an article on you next month. I just need to check a few details with you. Is that OK?
Martin:	Sure. Go ahead.
Alison:	What I wanted to know was did you set up in 1997?
Martin:	Actually, our first store opened in July '96 in Gateshead. We've been going for nearly ten years now.
Alison:	I didn't realize. Sorry. Where did you say the first store was?
Martin:	It's just outside Newcastle. Spelt G-A-T-E-S-H-E-A-D.
Alison:	Of course! And, let me see ... now you have over 200 stores in the whole of the country.
Martin:	350, actually, in the North. That's where we concentrate on at least for the moment. And we're due to open another six next year, in 2005.
Alison:	Wow! So you're obviously a successful operation. What about staff? How many people do you employ? I hear that you are a big employer as well. Perhaps the main employer in some parts.
Martin:	On average between forty and sixty in each store. So, at present, between fifteen hundred and two thousand people. Yes, we are an important employer in a number of towns in the North East.
Alison:	I see. So you are still expanding fast.
Martin:	We are. In fact, we now account for 7% of the food retail market and 2% in other sectors.
Alison:	That's pretty impressive. What do you put your success down to?
Martin:	In my view it's about ...

TEST FOUR   PART THREE

Woman: Good morning everyone. Thank you for coming. I want to say a few words about our business before you get started on your training programme. First of all, I want to thank you all for the part you played in making it such a successful summer season. As you know, the refurbishment of the lounges and the private dining rooms is complete and much admired by our guests. It was a difficult time for us all and I appreciated the way you made every effort to make our guests comfortable. It has been one of the best summers ever for Marlborough hotels. We've been particularly busy with weddings: one hundred and forty five this year, which makes it nearly four a week during the summer.

Our chef and his team have continued to attract customers with exciting and innovative menus. Well done, Jamie. We've actually seen a 25% increase in non-residents coming to our restaurants this month already. You must be doing something right.

I'd also like to welcome Jontje Lister who has recently joined us. Jontje is our new director of sales. She has come from London where she has had many years of experience in the hospitality industry.

Finally, I wanted to tell you about a new venture. We have decided that as a country hotel group we will be making a point of welcoming dogs (with their owners, of course!). I know some of you aren't keen on the idea, but just remember: dogs don't drop cigarette ends, spill coffee on the new carpets or sing loud songs in the early hours of the morning. So, I hope you will make our four-legged friends welcome in those areas of the hotel we have designated suitable.

Now I shall leave you in the capable hands of Keith. Enjoy your day!

TEST FOUR   PART FOUR

Man: I thought it might be useful today if I started by offering you a few words of advice about doing TV interviews. Many of you have already had this experience and it is becoming a more frequent part of the role of the chief executive and other company spokesmen. In the past the greatest challenge was to make a good speech. That was easy enough if you had someone good to write it for you. All you had to do was read what was written, smile now and again at the right places and you couldn't lose. Things have changed and the long, sometimes dull and boring speech to the shareholders is less important than the two-minute interview on national television.

And if you're speaking to a TV reporter, it's a big mistake to say something that sounds like you've made notes first. Explain what the company is doing but keep it short. You could say that your company is a forward-looking business but don't give too much detail or you'll sound like you are reading out of the brochure!

What you mustn't forget is that it may feel like you're having a conversation, but really it's more like a presentation. It's wrong to think that the interviewer wants to have a nice chat with you. If you do that, you may say more than you need to and that is sure to get reported back to the shareholders! Could be embarrassing, couldn't it.

Now you're probably used to giving your teams a lot of reasons why certain decisions have been made. Don't do that on camera. It's boring for the interviewer and you'll quickly lose the viewers, too. Instead, stick to the headlines, the decisions: that's all there's time for, believe me!

After all these warnings I still think that it's not all bad news if an interviewer wants to talk to you. Have something important to say and make it sound interesting. Make them want to interview you again and use the chance to tell thousands of people how good your company is and how they really need your products or skills.

Then there's the structure of the interview itself. I think it's good to have an opening sentence which sends the message you want people to hear. Don't just say 'It's nice to be here' or 'Thank you for inviting me'. Also, end the interview on a positive note if you can.

Then there are always those tricky questions. If a question comes up that you can't or don't want to answer, give yourself some time. Say 'Now that's an interesting question'. Then you can move on quickly to something you want to talk about. If you do it well, nobody will notice. If you do it badly it may sound like you are hiding something.

Finally, stay awake even after the interview has finished. Even if the light on top of the camera isn't on, take care. Don't relax until you are well away from the studio and driving home in your car.